Finding Purpose

Environmental Stewardship as a Personal Calling

Finding Purpose

Environmental Stewardship as a Personal Calling

Andrew J. Hoffman

Foreword by J.B. MacKinnon

Greenleaf
PUBLISHING

Published by Greenleaf Publishing Limited
Salts Mill, Victoria Road, Saltaire, BD18 3LA, UK
www.greenleaf-publishing.com

Cover by Sadie Gornall-Jones

Printed and bound by Printondemand-worldwide.com, UK

MIX
Paper from responsible sources
FSC® C004959

British Library Cataloguing in Publication Data:
A catalogue record for this book is available from the British Library.

ISBN-13: 978-1-78353-354-1 [hardback]
ISBN-13: 978-1-78353-372-5 [paperback]
ISBN-13: 978-1-78353-373-2 [PDF ebook]
ISBN-13: 978-1-78353-353-4 [ePub ebook]

It is true, I fear that others may have fallen into it, and so helped to keep it open. The surface of the earth is soft and impressible by the feet of men; and so with the paths which the mind travels. How worn and dusty, then, must be the highways of the world, how deep the ruts of tradition and conformity! I did not wish to take a cabin passage, but rather to go before the mast and on the deck of the world, for there I could best see the moonlight amid the mountains. I do not wish to go before now.

I learned this, at least, by my experiment: that **if one advances confidently in the direction of his dreams, and endeavors to live the life which he has imagined, he will meet with a success unexpected in common hours.** He will put some things behind, will pass an invisible boundary; new, universal, and more liberal laws will begin to establish themselves around and within him; or the old laws be expanded, and interpreted in his favor in a more liberal sense, and he will live with the license of a higher order of beings.

Henry David Thoreau, *Walden*, 1854[1]

Contents

Foreword

It is currently the fashion in business culture to speak of "disruption." Start-ups pushing the next generation of social media platforms, not much different from the last generation of social media platforms, describe themselves as a disruptive force. Gadgets with nothing more than raw consumeristic appeal are sold as disruptive technologies. Some firms even make oxymoronic claims of disruptive customer service.

This is all in the grand tradition of business and management books, which have long pickpocketed the language of rebellion and enlightenment. As a reader, you have surely been called upon again and again to "follow your dreams," "find your passion," and "go your own way," usually in defiance of some straw-man set of gray and tired mainstream norms. Most of these messengers, meanwhile, sell the same old dream of financial wealth, the same old passion for status, the same old longing for personal power. The language of environmental stewardship has been similarly abused. We hear tell of sustainable profits. Of green growth. Our homes—and our landfills—are increasingly awash with eco-friendly products.

It breeds a certain cynicism. One could be forgiven for siding with the many who believe that the movement for sustainability and green business, for all its buzz about innovation and "clean capitalism," remains more the problem than the solution to the great challenges of our times.

Andrew Hoffman would agree, and that's part of what makes this book different. Hoffman is an academic with experience in business and environmental stewardship: an unusual combination. His starting point is the simple truth that "without business there will be no solutions." He doesn't mean that only business can generate solutions, of course, but rather that the powers of ideation, production, and distribution that business represents are certain to play an essential role in making necessary changes to the way we live. Yet Hoffman also believes that business has not taken this role anywhere near seriously enough.

A new divide has opened in society in just this new millennium. On the one side are those who think that business as usual, or, as Hoffman puts it, business (almost) as usual, is still okay. On the other are those who recognize that there is now credible evidence that human civilization is at risk of collapse through the relentless pressure it places on planetary ecology. If you have picked up this book, then you are likely on, or at least glancing with curiosity at, the latter side of that divide. It's admittedly a frightening place to find yourself. On the other hand, it couldn't be more exciting.

If the evidence is correct, we need to change almost everything about the way we live; we need anything but business as usual. "Change everything"—I know, it's already a platitude on a T-shirt. Still, if we accept the evidence, then that platitude also happens to be true. We need to reinvent the way we move around, the buildings we live in, the way we eat, the stuff we buy. It won't be enough, though—not nearly enough—to overlay some matrix of green products over the culture of overconsumption that drives the rich-world economies of today. We'll also need to shift our relationships, our worldviews, and our innermost motivations. We'll need to change government, civil society, unions, and of course we will need to change business.

And so this book is first and foremost an invitation: Would you like to be a part of one of the greatest projects of imagination, perhaps the greatest ever, in human history? Again, if you're picking up this book, running your hand across its cover, flipping through its opening pages, then the answer to this question is almost certainly: of course you do.

I myself am not from the world of business, much less from academe. I'm a journalist and writer, mostly on ecological themes, and sometimes a reluctant activist, too. I first met Hoffman (well, he goes by Andy) when he invited me to speak to a green caucus of business professors; he was especially interested in the fact that I had recently set aside any pretense of journalistic objectivity and gotten arrested for protesting an oil pipeline development. He suspected that those who want to change business culture, who want to commit deeply to sustainability, need to tap into a similarly rebellious spirit. I suspect he's correct, and yet Hoffman also, in our conversation and with this book, convinced me that we don't necessarily need a movement from the boardroom to the blockades.

What are the alternatives to endless economic growth? What is the business model for products that last, without planned obsolescence? How do we make the price of products reflect their environmental and social harms? How do we measure economic success beyond sales and profits? What does business sell if it stops selling consumerism? Can corporations collaborate rather than compete? The search for the answers to these and other pressing questions can take place in the boardroom or the classroom, on the shop floor or in the ivory tower, and yet be as radical, as absolutely necessary, as any protest. That is, if the search is undertaken honestly, urgently, with courage, and with rigor.

Finding Purpose is a book about you, for you. That doesn't mean that it will pander to you. Most likely you are drawn to business and management: the creativity of it, the energy, the concrete contribution it can make to daily life, and, yes, the opportunities it offers. But Hoffman wants to guide you further than all of that. He asks that you critically examine your ambitions and frame them in the new context of the twin global crises of ecological degradation and social inequality. More challenging still, he asks that you look long and hard into your heart for the values to make a real and lasting contribution to environmental stewardship. Hoffman doesn't want to change your mind—he wants to change the direction of your life's journey.

And so this is one book, perhaps the first you will have read, that meaningfully asks you to follow your dreams, find your passions, and go your own way. I say "meaningfully" because it asks the hard questions first: Where do your dreams come from? What values form the foundation of your passions? Whose interests will be served as you go your own way? *Finding Purpose* is disruptive. Let it disrupt you.

J.B. MacKinnon
Vancouver, 2016

1

Introduction: Finding purpose

As a business professor, students often ask me where they should take their careers in order to have the most impact. They are expecting a straightforward answer: that they should work in finance in a large resource-extraction company, say, or in the advocacy department of a multinational non-profit organization. Instead, I am quick to tell them, "Wrong question: try again." The key question is one that only they can answer for themselves: "What were you meant to do with your life?"

This deeper exploration leads to the pursuit of a calling or a vocation, which is nothing more or less than your purpose in the world. We all have a goal or purpose to what we do. Where do you devote your energy? How much time do you spend with your family, or in the woods, or pursuing wealth? Are your relationships transactional or relational; that is, do you treat people and the natural world as a community that sustains and includes you, or merely as objects for achieving the success of your own pursuits? Are the answers to these questions internally generated, or are you listening to somebody else to decide what you are meant to be? Satisfaction in your life's work comes from knowing who you are and what you are called to do, and then sticking with your idea of how a life well lived is measured as you see where that spirit takes you.

This book opens with a quote from Henry David Thoreau, writing on his time at Walden Pond: "I learned this, at least, by my experiment; that if one advances confidently in the direction of his [sic] dreams, and endeavors to live the life which he has imagined, he will meet with a success unexpected in common hours."[2] The word "unexpected" is central to his message and reflects a belief that the pursuit of a calling is about opening up to the unknown. It will not be what we design, but instead the sum of what we experience. It will not be aimed toward a fixed end of stability and certainty, but a continuous pursuit of growth and awareness. A life well lived must be a creative endeavor, whatever form that creativity takes—whether it's finance, activism, painting, carpentry, teaching, raising a family, or writing a book. Chances are that, if we are genuinely open to the possibilities of a calling, we will find that satisfaction will come from some place far different from where we expected to find it.

I don't think of a vocation or calling as having to be God-centered—but it can be. And with all due respect to Joseph Campbell, it's not simply about "following your bliss."[3] It's about connecting to a purpose that is bigger than you and caring enough to devote your life, energies, passions, and love toward addressing it. It is a manifestation of your recognition and appreciation for the connectedness that we all have with the world, which includes our society, family, school, and natural world. Satisfaction comes not just from some inner feeling, but also from an assessment that what you are connected to and care about is being addressed. Satisfaction occurs in the world, not only in ourselves. It comes not from pleasure, but from meaning.

None of this is easy, and many do not even try to find their calling. Our commercial society wants us to believe that the pursuit of happiness that Thomas Jefferson wrote about in the Declaration of Independence has boiled down to "Miller Time" and consuming more stuff. Its central message is that your value is measured by what you accumulate and what others see, rather than by what you believe. College degrees, fancy cars, big houses, and happy Facebook posts: these can all become ways of projecting to people around you that you have worth. But they are not worth themselves. We live in a world of tremendous pressures for conformity and self-centeredness. I watch my students struggle with these pressures, most vividly at graduation time.

Many start their education with aspirations to eschew big salaries and work to pursue social good no matter their income. But when they look at the salaries that large consulting firms are giving to their peers, they begin to bend and yield. Some have little choice. College simply costs too much money, and they amass such large debt loads that they find themselves measuring their education in terms of return on investment. I watch as some accept high-paying jobs with the personal promise that they will leave once their student loans are paid off. But, all too often, their cost of living soon includes homes, cars, vacations, retirement accounts, health care, and their own children's ballooning college costs, creating chains that hold them back from keeping that promise. And I see those kinds of chains being formed earlier and earlier in people's lives. I sit on high-school scholarship committees and see students building their resumes from the seventh or eighth grade. The danger in teaching this practice so early is the concurrent lesson that the measure of your worth comes from outside and can be measured on a piece of paper. But your early training, debt load, cost of living, or resume should not stop you from pursuing a life's work of meaning. It may make that pursuit more challenging, but it does not make it impossible.

The lesson that I want people to take from this book, above all others, is what cannot be found in a textbook. There's pure joy when you take control of your life, defy the "rules" around you and take the risk to pursue your dreams and find work that you deeply connect with. As organizational development scholar Herbert Shepard wrote in his essay *A Path with a Heart*:

> We have been brought up to live by rules that mostly have nothing to do with making our lives worth living . . . Work is something you have to be compensated for, because it robs you of living. Play is something you usually have to pay for, because your play is often someone else's work . . . [But] a master in the art of living draws no sharp distinction between his work and his play, his labor and his leisure, his mind and his body, his education and his recreation. He scarcely knows which is which. He simply pursues his vision of excellence through whatever he is doing and leaves others to determine whether he is working or playing. To himself he always seems to be doing both.[4]

This book is written with this spirit in mind: of calling people to follow their own path. These essays are based upon my own work as a professor, teacher, and student, and upon the like-minded work of the people around me. I have watched and coached students in their twenties as they sought their true vocation, and I have done the same with mid-career professionals in their forties and fifties. It is never too late to consider the measure of your life's work based on internal meaning and purpose instead of external status and money.

Yet this is not only a book about finding your personal vocation. My goal in these essays—the personal calling that I am attempting to answer with this book—is to direct that work toward bringing about an environmentally sustainable world. Indeed, I believe that if many more of us do not do this, then we are doomed. The environmental challenges we face today are unprecedented and unlike any other challenge we have faced as a species since we emerged on this Earth. That we now unwittingly alter the global ecosystem imposes upon us a responsibility that we are ill equipped to handle. But to ignore that responsibility is to burden future generations with a hostile world for no other reason than that we were too selfish to care. We need to alter our social, political, and economic systems in ways that we have not yet imagined. The goal is not to tear down our current institutions like capitalism, as some suggest, but rather to amend them and bring them into line with geophysical realities. To do this, we need to instill in people a deep desire to use their abilities and influence to make the world a better place.

To my mind, there is nowhere that we need to instill these desires more than in business and education. The necessary changes that I am pointing to require new attention to notions of responsibility and purpose, which are not talked about enough in today's world, and are particularly absent from the training of those who go into business. We need to acknowledge the awesome power that businesses have in our world, and the awesome responsibility that business managers have in running them. They can bring the world to sustainability, or bring it to ruin.

To that end, the essays in Section I are written for business students; but they will resonate with the student in all of us. Those in Section II are written for business professionals; but we all participate in commerce and the market, whether as consumers, investors, employers, or employees.

Augmenting our approach to business, those in Section III are written for academic scientists; for we are all influenced by their scholarship, whether in the classroom or as consumers of information throughout our daily lives. And those in Sections IV and V are written for those who care about the world around them and the changes they want to see through their work. All are written for those searching for a calling, and all call for a change in our thinking that is based on being authentic about who we are and what we are meant to do with our life's work.

While technological and economic activity may be the direct cause of environmentally destructive behavior, environmental stewardship is not primarily about technological or economic activity. Instead, it is about our beliefs and values, the cultural norms and societal institutions that guide that activity. Many business students, joined by increasing numbers of experienced professionals, now hope to devote their education and careers to what is often called "green business." I thank them all for that. But I also believe that people need help and guidance to find a personal vision of how and where they can make the most difference. I am inspired and hopeful as I see so many people taking up the charge, finding a call to purpose by bringing environmental stewardship into their life's work. I see courageous people who strive to develop a sense of sacredness that allows them to be more authentic in resolving the conflicted value systems that create our environmental problems. The nature of their work has changed, from a career in which they earn a living to a vocation in which they express a set of deeply personal values in pursuit of goals far greater than themselves.

I hope you will take up this charge as well.

I
Life's Work as a Personal Vocation

2

Building hope

Hope is a curious word, one that is different than optimism. Optimism springs from some assessment that you are doing things that have worked in the past and therefore can say, "This is going to work." Hope is really a belief in the rightness of what you're doing. In Vaclav Havel's words, it is "the certainty that something makes sense."[5] Christopher Lasch says, "hope implies a deep-seated trust in life that appears absurd to those who lack it."[6] David Orr adds, "Optimism is the recognition that the odds are in your favor; hope is the faith that things will work out whatever the odds. Hope is a verb with its sleeves rolled up."[7]

When faced with the problems of our day, I am often asked if I am hopeful. My answer is always yes. The justification for that hope is the next generation that I see in my classrooms. The greatest joy, indeed the only real lasting legacy of a professor, is his or her students. They are my hope; they are all our hopes. Every new generation faces a new set of challenges left behind by the previous generation. For this new generation, environmental degradation stands as the ultimate challenge.

According to the UN Millennium Ecosystem Assessment, humans have changed Earth's ecosystems more in the past 50 years than in any comparable historical period. We have increased species extinction rates by up to a thousand times over the typical rate throughout our planet's history. Almost 25% of the world's most important marine fish stocks are depleted or over-harvested, while 44% are fished at their biological limit and vulnerable to collapse. As we extract the world's riches, we contaminate its atmosphere, altering our global climate through the unabated emission of greenhouse gases.

These impacts are not evenly distributed. According to the UN, the richest 20% of the world's population consume over 75% of all private goods and services, while the poorest 20% consume just 1.5%. Of the 4.4 billion people in the developing world (more than half of the world's population), almost 60% lack access to safe sewers, 33% have no access to clean water, 25% lack adequate housing, and 30% have no modern health services. And if that doesn't get your attention, then consider that the richest three people in the world have assets that exceed the combined gross domestic product of the 48 least developed countries.[8]

Many of the most critical solutions to these problems will, indeed they must, come from the economic market, including business, non-profit organizations, and governments. The market is the most powerful institution on Earth and, like it or not, business is the most powerful entity within it. Without business there will be no solutions. Business will design the next building we live and work in, food we eat, clothes we wear, automobile we drive, source of energy that propels it, and the next form of mobility to replace it.

It is exciting to see the speed with which sustainable business is catching on. You can now work on sustainability strategies, products, and operations; help write sustainability reports; and strive for positions like Chief Sustainability Officer. In the vast majority of cases, these opportunities did not exist ten years ago. So-called LOHAS—"lifestyle of health and sustainability"—consumers now represent almost 20% of the U.S. population, and can mobilize $290 billion in spending power each year towards sustainable products and services. Investment funds practicing impact investing, which aims to address social and environmental problems, can leverage just under $50 billion. The business world is changing.

But much more needs to be done. The solutions to the root problems we face must go far beyond an LED light bulb, windmill, or solar cell and reach deep into the complexity of our economy and society. On that front, too, I see signs of hope. We now live in a world where a 22-year-old part-time nanny can start an online petition of 300,000 signatures and force the Bank of America to cancel plans to charge debit card users a $5 monthly fee. Patagonia can ask consumers to buy their products used on eBay before coming to the store to buy new. Unilever CEO Paul Polman can say that we need to think on longer timeframes, that the concept of shareholder value has passed its "sell-by date," and that his company will no longer provide quarterly profit updates to shareholders.[9] And that's mild. Polman has also voiced the opinion that hedge-fund managers would "sell their own grandmothers if they thought they could make a profit" and that "we are entering a very interesting period of history where the responsible business world is running ahead of the politicians."

But we need to go still further. Even deeper than all of this, sustainability requires that we change how we conceive of ourselves as human beings, not merely as consumers; defining ourselves not by what we possess and what we buy but by who we are, what we believe, and—dare I say it—how we love the world around us, both human and non-human. Dwight D. Eisenhower once said, "We must avoid the impulse to live only for today, plundering for our own ease and convenience the precious resources of tomorrow. We cannot mortgage the material assets of our grandchildren without risking the loss also of their political and spiritual heritage."[10] That captures it.

We need profound cultural change to create a sustainable world. We need people who will think deeply, work diligently, and never give up. We need those people in all sectors of society, whether your path takes you to business, government, the nonprofit sector or elsewhere. As students (or students of life) taking the first steps on that journey, I hope and pray that you will develop the deep foundation necessary to have the persistence to keep trying, find the answers, and follow your path. Yet I also know that some of you, going forward, will struggle with the idea of "selling out" if you find yourself in a job that is not perfectly aligned with your personal vocation.

I ask you to reconsider the use of that term and apply more patience. I don't want you to measure the value of your worth in terms of where you are at any one point, but instead by the lasting legacy of decades of your life's work in whatever varied forms it takes. And I encourage you to think of that worth, not as a singular measure, but in concert with the careers of thousands, if not hundreds of thousands, of people who are engaged in a similar pursuit. The recognition that this is a collective effort, each person adding one piece to the composite whole, may help you keep the hope that is needed to continue in both good times and in bad.

When you get discouraged, and you will, I want you to recall these words by Thomas Edison: "Many of life's failures are people who did not realize how close they were to success when they gave up."[11] Think of a stonemason who has to hit the stone 100 times before it breaks. It's not the hundredth hammer strike that breaks the stone. It is the 99 that came before it. To make that hundredth strike with the hammer requires the persistence maintained by hope—your belief in the rightness of what you are doing, your certainty in your life's work.

3

Your theory of change

We all have a theory of change. When we ask our partner to change dinner plans for the evening, when we approach our professor to change the grade for a class, when we go into a company and try to change its sustainability strategy, we are working from a personal theory of what needs to change and why, and, importantly, how change takes place. That theory reflects how we see the world and how we engage with it. It defines who we are and how we will accomplish our life's work. For example, when I was a house builder before I was a professor, I learned that I could lead my work crew by fear, by being liked, or by being respected. For me, the best option was the third because it most closely fit who I was, and that was a major factor in my success in house building. As Heraclitus said, "Character is destiny."

I want to offer two reflections on the question "What is your theory of change?" The first begins with a quote from E.B. White, the author of *Charlotte's Web*: "Every morning I awake torn between a desire to save the world and an inclination to savor it. This makes it hard to plan the day."[12] I know I feel this same tension, and perhaps you do, too. We live in the world and are the product of it, and yet we want to push it in new directions. It's a hard balance to strike. Environmental stewardship is not just a contest between competing factions in society. In many ways, the contest is within each of us. In that sense, we are all in this together.

Yet people often apply an "us versus them" framework when they think about environmental problems. For example, I often hear it stated that we are addicted to fossil fuels. I have trouble with that metaphor. Addiction to drugs or alcohol is an illness that is an aberration from the norm. We know what is healthy behavior and we know what is not, in this case, because some people are addicts and some people are not. There is a measure of judgment when calling someone an addict.

But on issues of the environment, most notably climate change, we are all faced with the same challenge. In a sense, we are all addicts with the same malady, and there are no healthy people we can look to in order to gauge normal behavior. I think a better metaphor is a collective of people who are lost on a terrain they thought they knew. We know what addiction looks like when it is cured, but a group of people who are lost have no idea where to go. What we need are leaders who have a vision for a direction we might head in, but who also recognize that they are lost, as well.

And that leads me to my second reflection. A theory of change is more than a single question about how change happens. It must also reflect what we are changing and where we want to end up. A complete theory of change has three parts: a statement of the current reality, a desired future, and a path to get from one to the other. Let me take each of them in turn.

What is your statement of reality? As an example, over the past years the stock market has been reaching new heights. Is that the world you see? Or do you also recognize that unemployment remains frustratingly static and income inequality is widening? Do you see that sustainability is going mainstream, as evidenced by the proliferation of annual sustainability reports, chief sustainability officers, sustainability strategies, and sustainable products? Or do you recognize that many of the sustainability concerns that these efforts are supposed to resolve continue to get worse? Carbon dioxide levels are rising past critical thresholds. Man-made chemicals permeate our environment. A research scientist recently told me in a matter-of-fact fashion that there are measurable levels of the painkiller ibuprofen in the Mediterranean Sea. Think about that for a second. What kind of a world do you see?

I see a world in which we have entered what geophysicists call the Anthropocene, a geological epoch made distinct from all others by the global influence of human beings on the natural environment. Whether we like it or not, we now play a major role in the operation of many of the Earth's systems. Going forward, the fates of humankind and the planet are linked. This is a fundamental shift in how we think about ourselves and the world of which we are a part. It represents a challenge to deepen your education in sustainability, whatever your chosen field. Heed the warning of John F. Kennedy, who said, "All too often, we enjoy the comfort of opinion without the discomfort of thought."[13] Learn the science; understand the issues. Is climate change real? Are GMOs safe? Is nuclear power feasible? Should we geoengineer the ecosystem? Your statement of reality will be the foundation of your life's work.

What is your desired future? What kind of world do you want to help create? Where do you want to take us? I would hope that in seeing clearly the present reality, you will not stop at lamenting the current environmental and social imbalances. Instead, I challenge you to look beyond those problems to a future that is optimistic and attractive, one that includes a life of meaning, security, prosperity, and happiness for ourselves, our children, all of humankind, and all of nature. That is bold work. As the Welsh writer Raymond Williams once said, "To be truly radical is to make hope possible, not despair convincing."[14]

We have no shortage of cynics in today's world; that is not a resource that we need more of. In their essay *The Death of Environmentalism*, Michael Shellenberger and Ted Nordhaus point out that environmentalists tend to focus too much on the negative, and that the negative does not motivate people to follow a leader.[15] They point out that Martin Luther King, Jr., did not give a speech called "I Have a Nightmare," but rather "I Have a Dream." Leaders inspire people to action by creating a vision of a desirable future, not by scaring them with warnings that the end is near. What future do you see? I want you to think about that, and think about it hard. It will be the goal of your life's work.

What is the path that will take us from one to the other? This is where your theory of change starts to become clear. My hope is that you will reject convenient black-and-white, binary statements about the problems that we now face. That kind of lazy thinking is too much in vogue today. It is far too easy to proclaim that we have the truth and that others are not only wrong, but perhaps even malicious and evil. The thirteenth-century Muslim mystic and philosopher Ibn al-Arabi wrote:

> Do not attach yourself to any particular creed exclusively, so that you may disbelieve all the rest; otherwise you will lose much good, nay, you will fail to recognize the real truth of the matter.

While al-Arabi was talking about religion, his words can be applied to today's sustainability problems, which do not reside in one discipline (business, science, religion, or engineering) nor in one worldview (Democrat, Republican, libertarian, independent, or socialist). We need to work for the elusive middle way by understanding all sides of the issues we care about and the text and subtext of seemingly simple ideas; we must not pass judgment easily, but instead see the complex fabric—and therefore the complex solutions—with tolerance and compassion.

When I say "climate change," what do you hear? Some hear a global call to action based on scientific consensus and the need for a price on carbon pollution. Others hear the threat of more government, more power in the hands of environmentalists (whom they do not trust), restrictions on our freedoms, restraints on the free market, and even a challenge to their notion of God. These are their real concerns and they may all be triggered by this one idea: climate change. We need to be able to speak to and work with all kinds of people, even those whose worldviews we do not share, if we are to find common solutions to our common problems. There is no other way. Dogmatism and absolutism will not get us there.

To really lead people to a place we need to go, and some may be rightly afraid to go, you can't just know the right thing to do. You also need to feel it deeply. You have to feel it to believe it, for, if you don't believe it, you will never convince others to go where you seek to lead them. The way forward begins with you, within you. When I say that your theory of change must be founded in reality, I don't only mean that you need to be informed about the real world, but also that you must find a way to draw your inspiration from that world. I started this chapter with a few words from E.B. White. Let me now present the complete quote for you to ponder. "Every morning I awake torn between a desire to save the world and an inclination to savor it. This makes it hard to plan the day. But if we forget to savor the world, what possible reason do we have for saving it? In a way savoring must come first."[16]

4

Your model of leadership

I play in a casual summer golf league that is as much about beer-drinking banter as it is about hitting a golf ball. We don't generally talk about work. But one day Gregg, a fellow golfer, asked me, "Hey Andy, what do you do for a living anyway?" I told him that I was a professor and that I studied environmental issues. He asked, "Do you mean like climate change? That's not real, is it?" I told him that the science was quite compelling and that I believed that the issue was real. His next question was, "Are you a Democrat or a Republican?" I told him that I was an independent. He replied, "So what do you think about Al Gore?" I told him that I thought Gore had called needed attention to climate change but that perceptions of him unfortunately also helped to polarize it as a partisan issue.

I think about that conversation often. Gregg was not challenging my ideas; he was questioning my motives. He was trying to find out if he could trust me enough to listen to what I had to say—to figure out if I was part of his cultural community, his "tribe." I can imagine the hesitation he may have had in broaching this topic. Might I turn condescending and give him a science lecture, challenging his lack of deep knowledge on the issue while asserting my own? Would I begin to judge him and his lifestyle, critiquing his choice of car, house, vacation habits, or any one of the multitude of unsustainable activities that we all undertake? Might I begin to pontificate on the politics of the issue, complaining about the partisan divide between Republicans and Democrats or the corporate influence on our political system? These are all plausible and unpleasant scenarios that lead people to avoid discussing climate change. Indeed, according to a 2013 survey by the Yale Project on Climate Change Communication, two-thirds of Americans rarely if ever discuss global warming with family or friends.[17] It seems to have joined sex, politics, and religion as topics to be avoided in polite company.

Still, you have probably had a conversation—or, as is often the case, a heated argument—with someone about a similarly controversial issue. It's worth asking what we are trying to get out of these discussions. Are we trying to change "hearts and minds," or are we trying to make a point? Do we want to allow people a face-saving way to come to their own conclusions, or do we want to win, forcing them to acquiesce? In short, how do you want to lead people to hear your point of view? What is your personal model of leadership?

This is a question we all have to ask ourselves. While you learn about the work that needs to be done to bring about a sustainable world, you also have to learn about how people change the way they think. Richard Nixon once said:

> It is not enough for a leader to know the right thing. He must be able to do the right thing. The . . . leader without the judgment or perception to make the right decisions fails for lack of vision. The one who knows the right thing but

> cannot achieve it fails because he is ineffectual. The great leader needs . . . the capacity to achieve.[18]

How do you want to achieve? How do you want to lead? The answers will be as individual as each person reading this. Look around you to the leaders you admire; each has a different way of convincing, of leading. You have to find yours.

I, for example, have chosen the role of professor; I try to inspire my students through my teaching, and others through my written and spoken words as an academic. As with all roles, mine has both limitations and opportunities. Every professor comes to a point in their lives when they ask, "What is my legacy? What did I accomplish?" We professors can measure our impact by the number of papers we have published in academic journals, and how many times those papers have been cited, but that is not very satisfying. How did we change the way people think? We have no way to measure that. The answer to that question resides in our students and those who read our work or hear us speak.

In defining your own theory of leadership, you have to build the trust of those you are trying to influence, create a vision for the direction we might go, and understand how to overcome people's fears and convince them to follow. This is not easy!

In 2014, J.B. MacKinnon, author of *The Once and Future World,* was arrested for protesting a pipeline that energy company Kinder Morgan was attempting to build in British Columbia. In an article in *Orion Magazine* about the experience, MacKinnon described feeling a tremendous, almost overwhelming, sense of relief and delight after his arrest, because, as he said, "it feels good to be true to your conscience, to stand up for what you believe in."[19] He said that he was now sleeping well because he was taking action on what he called "not only a pipeline that will be snaking through British Columbia, but an ideology that is deepening our dependence on fossil fuels." One thing he wrote struck an especially personal chord with me:

> I'm a writer, but writing another article, proposing another idea, seemed unlikely to make a difference. The problem at this point is not a shortage of words or ideas. The problem is a shortage of people on Burnaby Mountain, at New York State's Seneca Lake, and in the many other places where local people are fighting a doomsday ideology playing out in their backyards.

That should sting a little for professors; it is a challenge to reexamine what we are doing and whether we should be do doing something differently. But reexamination is something we should constantly undertake. In so doing, we revitalize who we are and whether we are progressing in our life's work.

As I undertook this reexamination in light of MacKinnon's words, I found a funny irony in his message. While he said that writing will not change things, his writing touched me deeply. So his writing another article did make a difference, at least in me. Indeed, the very fact that he wrote about his arrest is a sign that he had not lost faith in the power of words, but instead was seeking, through his arrest, new and more powerful things he could say.

His words remind me of the awesome responsibility and opportunity we have for prompting change through our ideas, our ways of viewing the world, and our style of leadership. MacKinnon has found his; I have found mine; I hope you will find yours.

5

What do you believe?

Mark Twain once said, "The two most important days in your life are the day you are born and the day you find out why." Those of us who are professors had no involvement in that first day. But we hope we might have everything to do with the second.

During your years in college, you take classes and learn about the issues we face and the models and tools for understanding and addressing them. But the key to the second awakening that Twain describes is not just what you learn in class; it's also what you develop in the "in-between" time. Be sure to put yourself in the company of others who think and feel deeply about the same things that you do. This gives you a supportive community and culture as you lay the foundation for your calling or your vocation. But you will also need to put yourself in the company of those who think differently than you; they will test and help to clarify your beliefs. Finally, you need to find time for yourself. It is by taking time for reflection that you will discern what you truly believe.

The conviction of your beliefs is what will get you out of bed every morning and what will get you through the tough times. And you will have tough times. There are days when I have to turn off the radio if I hear another news story about climate change. There are days when I get discouraged that change is just too hard—when a U.S. Senator throws a snowball on the Senate floor to "prove" that climate change is not real, for example, or the government of Florida bans state officials from using the words "climate change." But I keep trying because I believe I must.

Let me offer three of my own beliefs that instill in me the purpose, hope, and responsibility that keep me going. As I describe mine, I invite you to consider what are yours?

I believe that there is far more to the natural world than what we can know or detect through our senses and empirical models, and that we have to protect it for reasons that are greater than our immediate and material needs or wants. I have done a lot of work at Yellowstone National Park, and what they are learning unexpectedly about the natural environment there continues to amaze me. For example, since the reintroduction of wolves in 1995, biologists have observed changes in the entire ecosystem in ways they never imagined. Among other surprises, who would have thought that wolves could change the course of rivers? Yet scientists have found that the presence of wolves prevents elk and deer from overgrazing riverside plants, which in turn stabilizes riverbanks and slows erosion.

Scientists studying red foxes within the park in winter, meanwhile, have recently discovered that the foxes catch 75% more mice—sometimes pouncing from as far as 20 feet away and through three feet of snow—when they are facing north.[20] This has led some to hypothesize that the foxes triangulate off the magnetic field of the Earth when pursuing their prey. These examples, and many more, remind us that there is so much that we do not know about the natural world.

More importantly, these examples remind us of the sacred and mysterious qualities in nature that will forever be beyond our grasp and compel us to protect it for its own sake. Rachel Carson captured this idea powerfully when she wrote:

> Contemplating the teeming life of the shore, we have an uneasy sense of the communication of some universal truth that lies just beyond our grasp. What is the message signaled by the hordes of diatoms, flashing their microscopic lights in the night sea? What truth is expressed by the legions of barnacles, whitening the rocks with their habitations, each small creature finding the necessities of its existence in the sweep of the surf? And what is the meaning of so tiny a being as the transparent wisp of protoplasm that is a sea lace, existing for some reason inscrutable to us—a reason that demands its presence by a trillion amid the rocks and weeds of the shore? The meaning haunts and ever eludes us, and in its very pursuit, we approach the ultimate mystery of Life itself.[21]

This quote comes from Carson's book *The Edge of the Sea*, and was excerpted as part of the eulogy at her funeral. You see that she has capitalized the word Life. She is calling forth something that demands our respect. So, while I may teach that we have to convince others to protect nature through self-interest, financial incentives, and pragmatic choices, I also believe we have to protect it for reasons that evoke words like sacred, divine, reverence, and love. This belief drives my devotion to my life's work.

I believe that not everyone has to have this reverence for nature; only a few have to possess it. For example, I am always shocked, amazed, and angry when I see garbage that a previous hiker has carelessly thrown along the trail. But I pick it up and believe that for every hundred people that may be so thoughtless, it takes only a small handful of us to make their carelessness right. I am reminded of the adage that a person who believes in something is a majority of one. I might add that the cold truth is that many people don't believe in anything. They simply follow the world as it exists without questioning the beliefs that they are fed—a particular concern when people don't challenge the continuous call for unrestrained consumption that we receive in every moment of every day in every medium. Yet even this understanding only underscores for me how important it is to be one of the people who know what they believe in. The idea that a relatively small number of committed people can solve problems that many others have helped to create gives me hope that we can address our environmental crises.

I believe that we have an obligation to use our gifts to leave the world better than we found it. In my faith tradition it is said that "For of those to whom much is given, much is required." I look at myself and I look at my students, and I see people to whom much is given: intelligence, opportunity, passion, wisdom, and vision. My belief that we have a responsibility to put those gifts to good use gives me persistence, especially when I get discouraged or tired. It forces me to look deep inside myself and muster the strength to keep trudging forward, to keep working, and to keep trying.

These are three things that I believe. Now I ask you: what do you believe? Do you know? Can you write three core beliefs down on paper? Do you have the courage to speak them out loud and to act on them? To know what you believe and to act on those beliefs is what will make your life's work have meaning. Anyone can figure out the "rules of the game" and devote their lives to beating the people around them in the competition for wealth and status. But that is not an original life, one based on a personal purpose. Once you come to believe in your purpose, in the reason that you were born, it is very hard to unbelieve it. It takes hold of you; it is something inside you that you can't shake. Find out what you believe. Don't just live the life you want to live; live the life you were meant to live.

6

Why do you care?

To protect something, we have to love it. And to love it, we have to take the time to appreciate its beauty and value. In 2014, I took some time to do just that. After giving a talk in California, I added three extra days to tour the Sierra Nevada and Yosemite National Park by motorcycle with an old friend.

Those three days reminded me of what sustainability is all about, allowed me time to reflect on my purpose and, at the most basic level, helped to restore my soul. As Robert Pirsig explained in *Zen and the Art of Motorcycle Maintenance*, experiencing the countryside on a motorcycle is a special way to explore.[22] It's not like seeing the world through the framed barrier of a windshield. The world is right there beneath your feet. You can reach down and touch it, and sometimes it reaches up and touches you—at one point, a bee landed inside my leather jacket and proceeded to sting me before I could come safely to a stop. As you ride, you feel the slightest change in temperature, and you smell everything: fruit groves, grape vines, pine forests, mountain waterfalls, barbeques, and dry fields. As you lean and balance through the switchbacks of the back roads, you are effortlessly part of the environment around you; riding a motorcycle is like turning thought into motion.

The weekend traversing Yosemite Valley was a visceral reminder that we need to preserve the wonders of our world for future generations, just as Teddy Roosevelt and Ansel Adams did before us. Our National Park system is still, as Ken Burns described it, "America's best idea," and our affection for it crosses political divides, geographic boundaries, and income levels.[23] But while we love nature, our relationship with it is not always easy, and the signs of that uneasy relationship were visible throughout the ride.

We stopped in the Hetch-Hetchy Valley to see the site that in the early 1900s inspired a national debate over whether or not to turn this breathtaking valley into a source of drinking water and electric power for the city of San Francisco. For U.S. Chief Forester Gifford Pinchot, the answer was clear: damming the valley would result in the greatest good for the greatest number of people. To the environmentalist and philosopher John Muir, the idea was sacrilege: Hetch-Hetchy should be left as it is for its own inherent value. I had taught and written about this epic battle for years, but had never seen the valley first-hand. Now that I have, I will speak differently about what it represents for the needs of humans and nature. And I will understand more personally the ways in which this historic clash manifests itself today.

For example, the signs of a water-stressed Central Valley were all too clear during my motorcycle tour. California was coming off its driest year since record keeping began in the 1800s, and the two prior winters had been abnormally dry as well. Farmers and conservationists were engaged in a heated war of words over the priorities for the limited available water. On the one side, the drought was forcing hundreds of thousands of acres to go unplanted with fruits, vegetables, nuts, and grains, and farmers were warning of a strained local economy and higher food prices. On the other side, the challenge of protecting fragile ecosystems and species had led regulators to allocate water to a tiny, endangered fish called the Delta smelt. Route 99 from Fresno to Merced was dotted with the signs of angry farmers who saw the water shortage as man-made and wanted the government to fix it by reallocating water from ecosystems to agriculture. To John Muir and Gifford Pinchot, this debate would have seemed all too familiar.

The clash over water was the downstream effect of what I saw in the highlands above; Sierra snowpack was just 18% of average for the time of year when my friend and I rode through. As we drove across the Tioga Pass Road at 9,000 feet, the shoulder was lined with snow banks as high as two feet. But this wasn't normal; this was the earliest in the year that the road had ever been open. The lack of snow assured that water in the Central Valley would remain insufficient for farmers for months or even years to come.

Crossing the Stanislaus National Forest, the fresh remnants of the 2013 Rim Forest Fire were evident everywhere. Caused by a hunter's illegal fire that went out of control, this was the third largest wildfire in California history (and the largest on record in the Sierra Nevada), consuming over 400 square miles of forest. Along the road, we saw massive trees that had been cut down, scorched and black on the outside but containing unharmed, high-quality lumber on the inside. Posted signs warned of the penalty for illegally removing the valuable timber. The Forest Service has proposed to allow salvage logging on about 30,000 acres of burned area and along 148 miles of high-use road in the burn perimeter. But conservationists oppose the removal of the timber on the grounds that it has a critical role to play as nature heals itself.

All of these experiences reinforce for me the importance of stewardship thinking: searching for ways to balance the needs of a strong economy with the goals of a healthy environment. Future generations will expect us to give them both. To see these tensions first-hand reminds me of the important work that we have to do. To see natural beauty first-hand fills me with the love and passion to actually do that work. The tensions represent problems we have to solve; the natural beauty tells me why we care. We can't address the first without the second.

II
Green Business as a Calling

7

Why green business?

In 2015, Apple CEO Tim Cook said, "Now more than ever businesses are in a position to help societies solve their greatest problems. The responsibility should not rest on governments alone. Whether we are talking about climate change or equal rights, the challenges we face are simply too great for businesses to stand on the sidelines."[24] Does this surprise you? Does it seem out of character for a business executive to talk about solving our environmental and social problems? It is not. Many companies have been searching for years to find ways to link their corporate strategy with the solution to our pressing societal challenges.

In fact, this kind of thinking is our only hope, most notably when it comes to climate change. Personal virtue is great, and I applaud anyone who chooses to make a deep commitment to living a green lifestyle. But if the market does not drive companies to do the same, solutions will never emerge on the scale necessary. The plain and simple truth is that no solution to these defining problems of our times will ever occur without the involvement of business.

This is why I urge you not only to find your calling in one or another aspect of business, with all the personal satisfaction and reward that may bring, but to seek that vocation in sustainable or "green" business. For the foreseeable future, business will be—must be—inseparable from the concept of sustainability, if the human project on Earth is to endure. The most exciting and important changes to how business is done will take place in this new context, and there will be tremendous opportunities for the creativity, leadership, deep thought, and committed effort that give meaning to a life's work.

How can we help move business in a mid-course correction that aims toward a more sustainable economy? The first step is to link environmental stewardship to the existing market metrics and logic—to frame the issue as a market shift, and one that is driven by standard business concerns for consumer demand, operational efficiency, and cost of capital. This can be termed "enterprise integration," and it's what companies are looking for today.

But the second and more important step is to recognize that the circumstances in which the economy operates are fundamentally different today than we understood them to be in the past. We have entered the Anthropocene, a new geological epoch in which human activity is recognized to play a significant role in the Earth's operating systems. We, as a species, have grown to such numbers, and our technology has grown to such power, that we are no longer merely drawing resources from our environment; we are altering and influencing the ecosystem on a planetary scale. This shift demands a change in societal views of not only the natural world and the human place within it, but of our need to collaborate on global problems. More directly, it demands a change in how markets are structured, and directs our efforts towards what can be termed "market transformation." While an understanding of enterprise integration can help you get your first job, a focus on market transformation can help you focus on the real solutions to our environmental problems over a lifetime. It will guide your life's work.

Given the way we have arranged human life on Earth, the central organizing structure for taking a positive place within the Anthropocene is the economic market. Never forget: the market is the most powerful institution on the planet, and business the most powerful entity within it. Businesses can transcend national boundaries and often possess resources that exceed those of many countries. You might lament that fact, but it is a fact. If business does not lead the way toward solutions for an environmentally sustainable, carbon-neutral world, there will be no solutions.

For example, business has the opportunity to move the public debate on climate change forward at a more rapid pace. This may sound surprising, given that many people see business, and especially big business, as obstructionist when it comes to climate action. Yet the strange truth is that scientific assessments by the Intergovernmental Panel on Climate Change (IPCC) and other organizations have still failed to convince a significant proportion of a wary public, and business assessments that climate change is a real concern can bring more of these people onside. If businesses spend money on it, then it must be true.

The messenger is as important as the message. To a certain segment of Americans, the environmental movement and scientific community are seen as left-leaning institutions whose ideas and arguments will always be suspect. But some businesses can be seen as "honest brokers" on this issue. Not businesses with vested interests in the outcome of climate debates, of course, such as oil and gas companies or renewable energy firms, but companies with no dog in the fight. Companies that just want to keep doing business the way they always have and now find themselves dealing with the challenges of a changing climate.

Not long ago, the *New York Times* posted an article entitled "Industry Awakens to the Threat of Climate Change," describing how Coke, Nike, the World Bank, and even the tycoons in Davos are looking at the physical impacts of climate change as a business risk with real dollars attached in the form of lost resources (e.g., water from droughts or agricultural products due to crop failures), disrupted supply chains (due to extreme weather), and other material issues.[25] This is the kind of news that shifts the public debate. When we see businesses pushing national governments to find policy solutions in Washington or at the Paris climate talks, or state legislatures to provide funding for coastal protections against sea level rise (such as in New York), then and only then will many in the undecided middle of America start to see climate change as real. As humans, we tend to act only when our personal interests are at stake, and for many people those personal interests are measured in dollars and cents.

The market must, and will, adjust to recognize the global nature of the issues we face. The next iteration of sustainable business practices, moving from enterprise integration to market transformation, will establish new norms of social and environmental behavior on a global level, translate those norms to the national and local levels, and develop solutions that are systemic in nature, rather than collections of siloed approaches. The end result will be shared but differentiated responsibilities for restoring the damages wrought by the past century of economic growth. This is not an assault on business; it is a shift in business as usual, as replete in market opportunities as any other form of disruption. It is the kind of atmosphere in which people in business have always rolled up their sleeves and gotten to work.

8

Green in the corner office

Green building used to be a movement of people in tie-dye shirts offering straw-bale and rammed-earth homes. Today, the field is populated by major corporations such as Siemens, GE, Turner, Trane, and Skanska, all drawn by real market returns. The U.S. Green Building Council estimates that up to 48% of new non-residential construction was green in 2014, which equates to a $145 billion investment opportunity.[26] They further estimate that 62% of firms building new single-family homes are doing more than 15% of their projects green and that that number will increase to 84% by 2018. Green building has become an ethical and economic no-brainer.

In the world of finance, Deutsche Bank estimates that the amount of assets under its management that are certified with a third party "green" label grew by €1.2 billion in 2014, raising the total to €4 billion. In 2015, Citibank announced a landmark commitment to lend, invest, and facilitate a total of $100 billion over the next ten years to finance activities that reduce the impacts of climate change, such as energy efficiency, urban infrastructure development, and green affordable housing. Citi's previous $50 billion goal was announced in 2007 and was met three years early in 2013. It would seem that environmentalists can now be found wearing grey pinstripe suits in the corner office.

This kind of news should warm a traditional environmentalist's heart. When we talk about green business today, we're not asking whether it "pays to be green." We're asking: how does it pay to innovate in green markets? We're talking about the challenge of innovation to capitalize on market shifts in resource and energy prices, consumer demand, capital costs, insurance premiums, and regulatory programs. Success depends on who does what, when, and how. Business is engaging with environmental issues for market reasons, not to "do the right thing" for moral reasons. The motivation is the profit motive, not a sense of guilt or shame.

To begin to grasp the systems-wide market shift that is turning the tremendous powers of the world's corporations to solving environmental problems like climate change, consider the following additional examples: Tesla has revolutionized the auto sector, bringing electric vehicles to market when many traditional auto companies said it was impossible; those naysaying competitors are now racing to catch up. Apple, Google, Uber, and Zipcar stand to further revolutionize the mobility industry, changing people's notions of what a car means in their lives. The energy sector, too, is going through a complete restructuring as we watch the demise of a utility model based entirely upon large centralized power plants, to be replaced by distributed generation of energy on rooftops, in farm fields, and in offshore installations. Smart grids, smart cities, smart cars, and social media tools to guide consumer choices are making our everyday lifestyles steadily more sustainable. These are the new realities that today's seasoned professionals and newly minted graduates alike want to be a part of.

I see it in my classrooms: students with no prior self-identification as being "green" seeking opportunities in the exploding greentech and green energy sectors. According to the UN Environment Program, 2015 saw a 17% increase in global green energy investments, reaching $270 billion.[27] Think for a moment about what might be accomplished with that kind of money. Similarly, the Brookings Institution estimates that U.S. clean-energy investment reached $36 billion in 2013, increasing by nearly 250% since 2004.[28] The U.S. Energy Information Administration predicts that 46% of new electricity consumption will come from renewables by 2030.[29] Seeing the opportunity and the need in this area, Bill Gates announced in 2015 one of the largest clean-energy partnerships in history, putting $1 billion of his personal wealth toward research into and deployment of new sources of carbon-free energy.[30] At the same time, a coalition of nations including the United States and India have agreed to double their research and development funding for clean-energy research. This is the market working to solve our environmental problems by fitting it within the existing logic of business. It does not require a "green" mindset to see the opportunities. It requires a business mindset.

Back in 2007, when the United States Climate Action Partnership—including businesses such as GE, Alcoa, DuPont, and PG&E—called for federal standards on greenhouse gas emissions, the *Wall Street Journal* dubbed them the "jolly green giants" and argued that they weren't trying to protect the environment but rather were acting in their own self-interest in promoting a regulatory program "designed to financially reward companies that reduce CO_2 emissions, and punish those that don't."[31] Well, stop the presses! The *Wall Street Journal* had just discovered that companies lobby for regulations that advantage them in the marketplace. But seeking advantage is what companies do. And any company that can foresee business opportunities in policies that are aimed at reducing carbon emissions or any other form of environmental protection is practicing what is expected of business managers.

There's an old Oklahoma expression that says, "If you're not at the table, you're on the menu." It warns that if you are not present at a dinner party, you will likely be a subject of gossip. The same adage can be applied to any company that sits on the sidelines as energy or climate policy is formulated: their competitors will be present to steer policy in their preferred direction, often at the expense of the absent firm. Regulations will burden certain companies, industries, and sectors more than others, and, likewise, will deliver advantage unevenly. The most advanced companies can even parlay their sustainability experience into an advisory role with governments. BP and Shell, for example, became savvy carbon-emissions traders in advance of any requirements, allowing them to become advisers to policymakers in the European Union. Many within the corporate sector in the U.S. see the same opportunities here. It's not "if" we will have policies to address climate change, but "when."

For those in business who still doubt the reality of climate change and are waiting for definitive scientific "proof," here's a cautionary tale: we still cannot state with scientific certainty that smoking causes lung cancer. The definitive U.S. Surgeon General report on the subject states that "statistical methods cannot establish proof of a causal relationship in an association [between cigarette smoking and lung cancer]. The causal significance of an association is a matter of judgment which goes beyond any statement of statistical probability."[32] The proof of a causal connection between second-hand smoke and lung cancer is even more difficult to make. Yet the scientific community recognizes that the preponderance of epidemiological and mechanistic data tell us that a link exists, and the general public shares that belief. Thus, we have regulations that limit tobacco sales and public smoking.

Similarly, there will be no scientific smoking gun on climate change. The global climate, like the human body, is too complex a system to model with complete accuracy (irrespective of the fact that a proper scientific study requires a "control"—another planet to compare this experiment to), and the standards for scientific certainty are just too demanding. Corporate executives should not confuse this lack of scientific certainty with a reason not to act. We will have to rely on the preponderance of evidence suggesting a prudent course.

The truth is that you can remain completely agnostic about climate science and still see it as a business issue. Boardrooms around the country are waking up to this fact. Even some stalwarts of climate skepticism—such as the American Enterprise Institute and ExxonMobil—are softening their opposition to curbs on greenhouse gas emissions. In 2014, former Ford CEO Alan Mulally declared:

> I firmly believe we are at an inflection point in the world's history as it relates to climate change and energy security. The time for debating whether climate change is real has past [*sic*]. It is time for a conversation about what we, as a society, intend to do to address it.[33]

This is not a new-found sense of social responsibility. It is hard-nosed business sense. The way Jim Rogers, former CEO of Duke Energy put it, you must avoid:

> . . . stroke of the pen risk, the risk that a regulator or Congressman signing a law can change the value of our assets overnight. If there is a high probability that there will be regulation, you try to position yourself to influence the outcome.[34]

With the price of oil fluctuating between highs of $105 a barrel and lows below $30 a barrel, energy management has become a material business issue. Companies want certainty in energy prices, and yet most have never really looked at energy efficiency. As Andreas Schlaepfer, head of internal environmental management at the leading global reinsurance firm Swiss Re, discovered, substantial reductions in emissions through energy conservation in buildings are quite easy. “If you’ve never focused on energy efficiency before, achieving 30% reduction is simple,”[35] he said. This leads to real and certain cost savings, both now and in the future.

Customers, too, are beginning to look for products and services that are environmentally friendly and energy-efficient. According to Casey Tubman, a brand manager at home appliance manufacturer Whirlpool, “In the 1980s, energy efficiency was number 10, 11, or 12 in consumer priorities. In the last four or five years, it has come up to number three behind cost and performance, and we believe these concerns will continue to grow.”[36] With some of the most energy-efficient appliances on the market, climate regulations translate into increased sales for Whirlpool.

Also, employees increasingly want to be associated with a company that has a strong environmental stance. According to one survey, 80% of young professionals are interested in securing a job that has a positive impact on the environment, and among MBA students 75% from top schools were willing to accept a salary lower by between 10% and 20% to work for a "responsible" company.[37] The outdoor gear and clothing company Patagonia credits its strong social mission with an astonishingly low turnover rate of between 6% and 7%, compared to an industry average of 43%.[38]

Even investors want to see action on climate change. In a recent survey, 50% of shareholders said that a company's mindfulness about the environment and society would make them more likely to buy their stock. JP Morgan and the Global Impact Investing Network have estimated the impact investing market—placing capital in enterprises with the explicit expectation of achieving both financial and social returns—to be $46 billion in 2014, up 20% from the previous year.[39]

Of course, not every business is in the business of change, and every market shift has winners and losers. Some industries, such as coal, will find it difficult to thrive in a market environment that is concerned about climate change. But that shouldn't stop today's students and managers from searching for solutions in whatever organization they find themselves. Reflecting this pragmatic tone, one of my students, Doug Wein, put it this way: "If you've got an 18-wheeler flying down the highway, running over property, disobeying the road signs, and causing general havoc, you can try to set up road blocks, throw rocks at the windows, or try to slash the tires. Or you can climb into the cab and try to talk the driver into slowing down. Better yet, you can grab the wheel and slow it down yourself."

9

Business (almost) as usual

F. Scott Fitzgerald once wrote "The test of a first-rate intelligence is the ability to hold two opposing ideas in mind at the same time and still retain the ability to function."[40] Environmental stewardship challenges us to do the same—we must work to solve the problem while, at the same time, our efforts are only slowing, not reversing, our damage.

Sustainability has gone mainstream. Firms develop sustainability strategies, scholars pursue sustainability as a field of research inquiry. Consumers buy green products, drive low-emission cars, and are bombarded with marketing campaigns that incorporate environmentalism. The world, it would seem, is on the road to a sustainable future.

It is not. In fact, things are getting worse. Increasing levels of greenhouse gases continue to alter our global climate and show no signs of abating. Fossil fuel use continues to grow, leading us to reach ever deeper into the Gulf of Mexico or the Arctic, harvest oil from tar sands in Canada, and hydrofrack natural gas from shale deposits in the United States. Unrestrained fertilizer runoff has led to toxic algal blooms in the Great Lakes and a vast dead zone at the mouth of the Mississippi River. We continue to destroy ecosystems in our never-ending thirst for development and natural resource extraction. All of this is fed by a steady diet of consumer culture that compels us to acquire more stuff, regardless of the environmental impact it creates, which is very often beyond the awareness of each individual user. So, despite the mainstreaming of sustainability, we are not becoming more sustainable. How can that be?

The answer lies in who is defining sustainability and the agenda they are pursuing. While the 1987 Brundtland Commission Report, *Our Common Future*, popularized sustainable development as "development that meets the needs of the present without compromising the ability of future generations to meet their own needs," the concept has been under reconstruction ever since.[41] Companies, governments, non-governmental organizations, foundations, research-rich universities—you name it, they have redefined sustainability for their own purposes. But business, and most notably groups such as the World Business Council for Sustainable Development, has taken the strongest role. Sustainability has been framed in the language most palatable to Western business, to fit within the existing rules of the Western market. It has become a slave to business interests—often merely a label for business-as-usual strategies as opposed to planet-first motives. This demoted and diluted notion is far from sustainability's meaningful intent.

Most corporate sustainability efforts are built upon the notion of eco-efficiency, or the idea that we can optimize industrial processes to reduce environmental insults, when in fact it is the processes themselves that are unsustainable. Reducing the carbon footprint of the production of a new widget has little benefit when we are consuming ever more widgets. Efficiency is a central tenet of the economic models used to devise public policy and business strategies, because efficiency is a key driver of competition and growth. And yet, like growth, efficiency cannot be the long-run strategy for sustainability. There simply isn't enough Earth to allow for perpetual growth in material terms, and certainly not if growth adds to, rather than reduces, social inequality.

To call eco-efficiency a sustainability strategy is misleading; in fact, it is only a strategy to reduce unsustainability. And as industrial ecologist John Ehrenfeld often points out, reducing unsustainability is completely different from creating sustainability, and we have to move from the former to the latter.

Don't read this as being entirely opposed to the sustainability efforts taking place within the corporate sector. Actions that reduce unsustainability are important—without them, the velocity at which we are approaching ecological system collapse would be much higher. Still, it is a strategy that gets the big picture mostly or completely wrong. The road to high profits for corporations always has been to push, whether intentionally or not, the hidden social and environmental costs of their products onto consumers and others, and present-day corporate sustainability strategies continue to do exactly this same thing. They ignore the systemic effects of what they do to produce and market their goods and services. Further, the way they advertise and publicize their programs lulls the public into believing that the firms are taking care of our collective future.

At best, this approach can produce only incremental, Band-Aid solutions—it will not solve the unsustainability problem at its roots. A corporation cannot become sustainable in isolation.

Sustainability is a property of the whole interconnected system in which the firm is situated: other firms, customers, the natural environment, regulators, banks, and so on. What matters is the health of that worldly system, not the health of any particular enterprise within it.

Corporate Social Responsibility, or CSR, which has become the measure of how businesses care about people and the environment beyond the usual economic factors, tends to be either oxymoronic or hypocritical. The CSR programs at companies such as Walmart, which have a strategy to grow in the name of efficiency and at the expense of local merchants, suppliers, and workers, are inconsistent with the vision of sustainability. Such efforts hold humans only as instrumental factors of production—commodities. Immanuel Kant said, "Act in such a way that you treat humanity, whether in your own person or in the person of any other, never merely as a means to an end, but always at the same time as an end." When we ignore this moral imperative, true sustainability struggles to burst forth. Most CSR programs merely balance the harms done in one place with token beneficence in another.

When we talk about the mainstreaming of sustainability, we also need to ask if sustainability stands up to the global-equity test. Can we consume and develop our way to a sustainable future at the global level? How often do we have to repeat the oft-told truism, which would be cliché if it weren't still so acutely relevant, that if everyone lived by the standard of a person in the U.S., the world would need the resources of seven planet Earths to survive? For those in the developed world, this fact is insulting. The affluent 20% of the world (who hold 86% of global wealth) appear unwilling to accept a reduced standard of living. Are they then asking the poorest 20% of the world's population (with their 2% of the global pie) to accept reduced growth rates and an arrested journey to an improved quality of life?

It's simple mathematics. For development to be truly sustainable at a global level, two things need to be addressed: the rich need to consume fewer resources, and economic and human development for the poor must be accelerated. This is the global-equity test for us all. The reality is that, when viewed from the developing world, sustainability as we know it today leaves a lot to be desired.

Take Indonesia, for instance, where universities have progressive environmental and social studies that clearly define the problems and propose enticing solutions, yet sustainability remains elusive. As is the case in much of the world, Indonesia's sustainability agenda is derived from the triple-bottom-line concept, often depicted as the nexus of three interlocking circles representing the economic, social, and environmental spheres. Yet the way that development has been pursued in Indonesia suggests a giant Mickey Mouse head: a big circle for the economy, and two small (and separate) circles for social and environmental sustainability. The practical result of this Mickey Mouse development model is increasing community protests, labor riots, and human rights abuses, all exacerbated by accelerated environmental degradation.

Without a global equity test, sustainability is often merely a façade to maintain the status quo. The continual focus on the business case for sustainability means that the underlying rules of development—economic growth and wholesale consumption—have not changed. Nor have the rules of the global North–South divide between rich and poor nations. This is a call for the developed world to learn from the developing, where social networks (in their original iteration) and a sense of community are still the fabric that weaves society together, and where consumption is still subservient to people and community, not vice versa. We cannot overlook the contribution of traditional cultures to the "new" sustainability paradigm.

In the end, the phrase "corporate sustainability" has come to mean a condition in which the corporation prospers for a long time. This is not what it was meant to refer to, but there it is. In our drift toward reducing unsustainability, we have lost our vision. True sustainability still has not entered our consciousness, in spite of the ubiquity of the term and its cousin, "green." Sustainability in its truest sense is not some new technology, triple-bottom-line metric, or series of steps that corporations and consumers adopt. We need to look beyond the economic and technological aspects of sustainability and focus instead on its behavioral, cultural, and institutional underpinnings. In fact, there is strong reason to be skeptical of "sustainable technology" and products that fool us into thinking we are solving the problem, when all we've probably done is figure out how to make the wrong thing last longer. What we need to learn is to make not just any thing, but the right thing, and make it to last.

No matter how much green business talks about what it is doing for sustainability, we remain stuck in the world of what John Ehrenfeld and I call, in our book *Flourishing: A Frank Conversation about Sustainability*, Business (Almost) As Usual.[42] It's different from Business As Usual, but it is not the kind of paradigmatic or transformational shift that is necessary to address health, well-being, community-building, interconnectedness, and all the other parts of the vision of true sustainability. Returning to the words of John Ehrenfeld, "at this moment in time, almost everything being done in the name of sustainability entails attempts to reduce unsustainability." But reducing unsustainability does not and will not create sustainability.

10

Capitalism and markets must evolve

There are two extremes in the debate over capitalism's role in solving our present climate change problem. On the one hand, some people see climate change as the outcome of a consumerist market system run rampant. On the other, some people have faith in a free market to yield technological solutions to the crisis, through a combination of renewable energy sources, energy and resource-use efficiency, and methods of cleaning up carbon pollution. Some even see climate policy as a covert way for bigger government to interfere in the market and diminish citizens' personal freedom. Caught between these two extremes, the public debate takes on its usual black-and-white, conflict-oriented, unproductive, and basically incorrect form.

Such a debate feeds into a growing distrust that many have for capitalism. A 2013 survey found that only 54% of Americans had a positive view of the term, and in many ways both the Occupy and Tea Party movements share a similar lack of faith in the macro-institutions of our society to serve everyone fairly.[43]

The former focuses its ire at big business, the latter at government, and both distrust what they see as a cozy relationship between the two.

This polarity also feeds into the culture wars that are taking place in our country. Studies have shown that conservative-leaning people are more likely to be skeptical of climate change, due in part to a belief that this would necessitate controls on industry and commerce, a future they do not want. Indeed, research has found a strong correlation between support for free-market ideology and rejection of climate science. Conversely, liberal-leaning people are more likely to believe in climate change, in part because proposed solutions are consistent with resentment toward commerce and industry and the damage they cause to society.

Our current, binary framing of the climate challenge masks the real questions we face, both in terms of what we need to do and how we are going to get there. Nonetheless, there are serious conversations taking place within management education, research, and practice about the next steps in the evolution of capitalism, driven not only by climate change, but by recent financial crises, growing income inequality, and other serious social issues.

Capitalism is a set of institutions for structuring our commerce and interaction. It is not, as many think, some sort of natural state that exists free from government intrusion. It is designed by human beings in the service of human beings and it can evolve with the changing needs of human beings. As Yuval Levin points out in *National Affairs* magazine, even Adam Smith argued that the rules of the market are not self-legislating or naturally obvious, and that the market is a public institution that must have rules imposed upon it, preferably by legislators who understand its workings and potential benefits.[44]

It's worth noting that capitalism has been quite successful. Over the past century, the world's population increased by a factor of four, the world economy increased by a factor of 14 and global per capita income tripled. In that time, average life expectancy increased by almost two-thirds due in large part to advances in medicine, shelter, food production, and other amenities provided by the market economy. Over time, regulation has evolved to address emergent issues such as monopoly power, collusion, price-fixing, and a host of other flaws in the functioning of markets. Today, one of the most urgent of those flaws is the fact that the market, as currently structured, is the major driver of climate change.

The question is not whether capitalism works or doesn't work. The question is how it can and will evolve to address the new challenges we face as a society. As the *New York Times* columnist Anand Giridharadas has argued, "Capitalism's rough edges must be sanded and its surplus fruit shared, but the underlying system must never be questioned."[45]

These rough edges need be considered within the context of the underlying theories and models used to understand, explain, and set policies for the market. Two that have received significant attention are neoclassical economics and principal–agent theory. Both theories form the foundation of management education and practice and yet are built on extreme and rather dismal simplifications of human beings as largely untrustworthy and driven by avarice, greed, and selfishness.

Writing in the *McKinsey Quarterly*, Eric Beinhocker and Nick Hanauer had this to say about the neoclassical vision of humans as isolated individuals, each acting in nothing more than his or her own rational self-interest:

> Behavioral economists have accumulated a mountain of evidence showing that real humans don't behave as a rational *Homo economicus* would. Experimental economists have raised awkward questions about the very existence of utility; and that is problematic because it has long been the device economists use to show that markets maximize social welfare. Empirical economists have identified anomalies suggesting that financial markets aren't always efficient.[46]

Principal–agent theory is equally problematic. It is built on an assumption that a dilemma occurs when one person (the "agent," or manager) makes decisions on behalf of another person (the "principal," or owner), because the agent is inevitably motivated to act in his own best interests rather than those of the principal. Lynn Stout, writing in the Brookings Institution's *Issues in Governance Studies*, goes so far as to say that the model is quite simply "wrong." Stout, a Cornell professor of business and law, argues that the notion plainly does not capture "the reality of modern public corporations with thousands of shareholders, scores of executives and a dozen or more directors."[47] To boil down the operations of the modern corporation to such a dyadic and mercenary relationship does not mirror the real-world motivations and actions of most managers.

The most pernicious outcome of these theories is the currently dominant idea of what corporations are for. If I asked any business school student (and perhaps any American) to complete the sentence, "the purpose of the corporation is to . . . ," they would parrot back, ". . . make money for the shareholder." But this is a rather recent idea that began to take hold within business only in the 1970s and 1980s. Most executives would tell you instead that companies transform ideas and innovation into products and services that serve the needs of some segment of the market. Where neoclassical economist Milton Friedman would have us believe that the purpose of the corporation is to serve the shareholder, management theorist Peter Drucker countered that the purpose of the corporation is to serve the market and the customer. Going further, Paul Polman, CEO of Unilever, says that "Business is here to serve society."[48] Profit is merely the metric for how well they do that.

The problem with the widely held notion that a corporation's sole purpose is to serve shareholders is that it leads to many other undesirable outcomes. For example, it inspires an increased focus on quarterly earnings and short-term share price swings; it encourages a decreased focus on long-term investment and strategic planning; and it rewards only the type of shareholder who, in the words of Lynn Stout, is "shortsighted, opportunistic, willing to impose external costs, and indifferent to ethics and others' welfare."

Similar critiques are increasingly made of the ways that we gauge the health of the economy. One of those metrics is the discount rate, the idea that a dollar in the future is worth less than a dollar today and must therefore be discounted. But economist Nicholas Stern stirred a healthy controversy when he used an unusually low discount rate (roughly 0.1%) when calculating the future costs and benefits of climate change mitigation and adaptation. By using such a low rate, the costs—and therefore the urgency—were higher than other economic analyses have calculated. Justifying this decision, he argued that there is an ethical component to this metric's use. For example, a common annual discount rate of 5% leads to the conclusion that everything that occurs 20 years out and beyond is worthless. When gauging the response to climate change, is that an outcome that anyone—particularly anyone with children or grandchildren—would consider ethical?

The foremost indicator of national economic progress is gross domestic product (GDP), a measure of all financial transactions for products and services. But one problem with GDP is that it does not acknowledge, nor value, a distinction between those transactions that add to the well-being of a country and those that diminish it. Any activity in which money changes hands will register as GDP growth. GDP treats the costs of recovery from natural disasters as economic gain; GDP increases with polluting activities and then again with pollution cleanup; GDP treats all depletion of natural resources as income, even when the depreciation of those capital assets can limit future growth.

A second problem with GDP is that it is not a metric dealing with true human well-being at all. Instead, it is based on the tacit assumption that the more money and wealth we have, the better off we are. But that's been challenged by numerous studies. As a result, Nicolas Sarkozy, while president of France, commissioned Nobel laureates Joseph Stiglitz and Amartya Sen to examine alternatives to GDP as the principal gauge of the economy. The commission's report recommended a shift in emphasis from simply the production of goods to a broader measure of overall well-being that would include categories such as health, education, and security. It also called for greater focus on the societal effects of income inequality, new ways to measure the economic impact of sustainability, and ways to include the value of wealth to be passed on to the next generation. Similarly, the king of Bhutan has developed a GDP alternative called Gross National Happiness, which is a composite of indicators that are much more directly related to human well-being than monetary measures.

All of this, and the dire failure of capitalism to solve many of the environmental challenges that it has created, has led some to argue for the creation of a new system to replace capitalism. For example, Naomi Klein, writing in *The Nation,* calls for "shredding the free-market ideology that has dominated the global economy for more than three decades."[49]

But the nature of social change never allows us the clean slate that makes sweeping statements in favor of radical change attractive. Every set of institutions by which society is structured evolved from some set of structures that preceded it. Paleontologist and baseball fan Stephen Jay Gould made this point powerfully with his essay *The Creation Myths of Cooperstown,* in which he pointed out that baseball was not invented by Abner Doubleday in Cooperstown, New York, in 1839.[50] In fact, "no one invented baseball at any moment or in any spot." It evolved from games that came before it. Similarly, Adam Smith did not invent capitalism in 1776 with his book *An Inquiry into the Nature and Causes of the Wealth of Nations*. Smith was writing about changes that he was observing and which had been taking place for centuries in European economies, most notably the division of labor and the improvements in efficiency and quality of production that were the result.

In the same way, we cannot simply invent a new system to replace capitalism. Whatever form of commerce and interchange we adopt must evolve out of the form we have at the present. There is no other way.

But one particular challenge of changing capitalism to address climate change is that, unlike the market of Adam Smith's proverbial butcher, brewer, or baker who provides our dinner out of the clear alignment of his or her self-interest and our needs, climate change breaks the link between action and outcome in profound ways. For the most part, we do not learn about climate change through direct experience. We cannot feel an increase in global mean temperature; we cannot see, smell, or taste greenhouse gases; and we cannot link an individual weather anomaly with global climate shifts.

Instead, a real appreciation of the issue requires an understanding of large-scale systems through "big data" models. Moreover, an appreciation of these models requires deep scientific knowledge about complex dynamic systems and the ways in which feedback loops, time delays, accumulations, and nonlinearities operate within the climate system. The evolution of capitalism to address climate change, therefore, must in many ways be based on trust and faith in stakeholders outside the normal exchange of commerce. To get to the next iteration of this centuries-old institution, we must envision the market through all components that help to establish the rules: corporations, government, civil society, and, importantly, scientists. Capitalism can, indeed it must, evolve to address our current climate crisis, but this cannot happen through either wiping clean the institutions that presently exist or relying on the benevolence of a *laissez faire* market. It will require thoughtful leaders creating a thoughtfully guided market.

11

Dark green or light green?

The rift between climate believers and deniers is one of the important schisms of our times, but it is not the only one. A schism also exists between two camps within the environmental movement. On the one side are what the futurist Alex Steffen calls "dark green" groups, such as Greenpeace USA and Friends of the Earth, which seek radical social change to solve environmental problems, most often by confronting the corporate sector.[51] As Steffen explains it, they tend to be critical of consumerism, and sometimes even of the industrialization that has produced much of modern life as we know it. On the other side, the "bright green" groups, such as The Nature Conservancy and the Environmental Defense Fund, work within the market system, often in close collaboration with corporations. Their mission, Steffen writes, is "to use innovation, design, urban revitalization, and entrepreneurial zeal to transform the systems that support our lives."

Steffen coined these terms in 2003. More than a decade later, this division has only widened. Books with titles like *Green Inc.* and *Hijacking Sustainability* criticize the bright greens as having been co-opted by companies to help greenwash environmentally damaging activities. Bright greens, meanwhile, dismiss dark greens as out-of-touch radicals who only complicate the environmental agenda with their utopian demands and sometimes extreme tactics, such as liberating mink from fur farms, ramming whaling ships, or burning down genetic engineering labs and crops. This antagonism is to be expected, but the reality is that the two sides are mutually dependent. They both need each other to accomplish their goals.

Scholars who have studied the civil rights movement and other periods of change argue that more extreme groups within a movement actually help the moderate, consensus-building groups through what sociologist Herbert Haines called a "radical flank effect." When radicals pull the tail of the political spectrum further in one direction, they shift the center of the debate and make previously radical groups seem moderate. Think of Martin Luther King. When he first began to speak out, his message was too much for many white Americans to accept. When the more militant Malcolm X became a public figure, he pulled the political flank so far to the left that King became palatable. Mainstream America was suddenly prepared to hear King's now "moderate" message. As an example from the environmental movement, we might recall Russell Train, the second administrator of the U.S. Environmental Protection Agency, who once quipped, "Thank God for [environmentalist] Dave Brower; he makes it so easy for the rest of us to be reasonable."

Moderates help move change along through incremental gains, while more radical groups often set the agenda and become the standard bearers for a movement's transformative goals. Radicals focus on the deeper, core issues of the movement; moderates find ways to give the movement widespread appeal and pragmatic action. Together, the two seemingly different branches really form a broad and connected spectrum. Sometimes this has been described as a tension between confrontation and collaboration, or purity and pragmatism. The environmental movement needs both.

Green business tends toward the bright green end of the spectrum. That's pragmatic, but it can be dangerous, too. As green goes mainstream, it fades. When Clorox introduces its new line of Green Works cleaners, GE develops wind turbines under its Ecomagination program, Toyota develops its Hybrid Synergy drive train, or Matsushita increases lithium-ion battery production, these are not examples of green products; they are examples of companies attacking new and profitable market segments and hastening a market shift that's already under way. I can see green, as we have known it, fading in my business classes on environmental strategy as they explode from the domain of a fringe group of environmentally minded students to attract mainstream business students who simply see environmental issues as critical to corporate success.

That's why, in the end, even green business needs those sometimes troublesome dark greens. They continually warn us against compromise and push the frontier of environmental issues. Dark greens keep our eye on the urgency of issues like climate change, ecosystem destruction, water scarcity, and, most importantly, the flaws in our social and economic systems that create these crises. Where the pragmatism of bright greens can lead to a perception that progress is being made, dark greens remind us that the problems worsen, that time is limited, and solutions must be bolder than politics and economics may presently allow.

Unfortunately, dark greens are losing their power and voice. They're becoming marginalized, not only by their own activities, but also by the way they're often cast in extreme relief against the more moderate bright greens. In my own research, I have found a strong positive correlation between the size of an environmental organization's budget and the number of corporate ties it engages. The implication is obvious: because bright greens actively engage with corporations, they have more money and therefore more influence than dark greens. This is bad for the movement as a whole.

We need more dark greens, and more support for dark greens, in the world of green business, because the dark green message is needed now more than ever. Here's why: only an appeal to deeply held morals and values can move us where we truly need to go. Only when the emission of CO_2 is seen as morally or ethically wrong (or even as a sin) will we be able to deal with climate change with the same finality with which we sought to abolish slavery. The breadth and depth of the necessary shift—both slaves and fossil fuels have historically been inexpensive sources of energy with terrible social or environmental costs—makes this comparison apt.

The solutions to environmental destruction are not merely technological, economic, or political. In their book *Beyond the Limits*, environmental writer Donella Meadows and her co-authors argue that the way to prevent the environmental collapse predicted by their models "will have to be, above all, a societal transformation that permits the best of human nature rather than the worst to be expressed and nurtured."[52]

Real sustainability demands that we be highly critical of modern culture. It challenges us to move away from our present-day "culture of commerce," in which consuming has become a central tenet. It recognizes that this path to today's "good life" is a mirage, an unfulfilled promise, and a myth based on the dominant notion of *Homo economicus,* or Economic Man—an archetypal human being who measures value in purely economic terms, sees relationships as primarily transactional, and extols wealth maximization as the ultimate goal in life.

Addressing sustainability fully and meaningfully requires a fundamental shift in the way we think and the way we organize our society. We don't need electric cars and cloth diapers so much as we need a deep shift in our values that is on a par with the Reformation, the Renaissance, the Enlightenment, the Industrial Revolution, or the Digital Revolution. All of these involved changes in the way we think about ourselves, each other, and the world around us. This notion of sustainability demands, in the words of Aldo Leopold, the early twentieth-century ecologist and author of *A Sand County Almanac*, an "internal change in our intellectual emphasis, loyalties, affections, and convictions."[53] Change that is short of that scale simply will not be enough.

III
Reclaiming the Role of Academia

12

Making bricks versus making change

Academic research has become a field of brick makers. This was the theme of a letter by Bernard K. Forscher published in *Science* magazine in 1963, and his critique, in the form of a parable, is even more relevant today.[54] Forscher lamented that academic scholarship had become fixated on generating lots of pieces of knowledge—bricks—and was far less concerned with putting them together into a cohesive whole. In time, he said, brick-making would become an end in itself.

His metaphor aptly depicts today's reality, and the quality of public and political debate suffers as a result. Academic success lies in publishing academic journal articles that make incremental contributions to theory, not in summarizing the broader contributions of the community of scholars. Specialization, not generalization, is the signal of academic rigor. The conventional rules of academic tenure and promotion all steer in that direction. With some notable exceptions, few scientists are building an edifice, telling a whole story as it presently exists, and determining what new "bricks" of information may be necessary to tell the next chapter in that story.

It is time for that to change. It is time to build a meaningful whole from the large and growing body of research in the physical and social sciences on a host of pressing issues: climate change, nanotechnology, nuclear power, autism and vaccines, GMOs, stem-cell research, and more. Academic scholarship can and must enter more fully into the national debate on these issues, and other academics must build on that scholarship.

It is equally crucial that academic knowledge be made available and accessible to an educated public that can put the insights of this research to use. Again, this is not something for which academe rewards scholars and scientists. Academics are encouraged to build bricks that are used by other brick-makers. The predominant focus on A-level journals feeds what some have called an academic "theory fetish," in which practical relevance takes a back seat to theoretical rigor, and empirical evidence is used to inform theory, rather than the other way around. Russell Jacoby, a professor of history at UCLA, warned in his book *The Last Intellectuals* that the increasing insularity of individual academic fields "registers not the needs of truth but academic-empire building."[55] Academics find themselves talking to ever smaller and narrower audiences of other academics, using a language that others do not understand, publishing in journals that no one outside the discipline reads, and asking questions the public doesn't care about. Whether this work actually results in real-world change is a question that is rarely, if ever, asked; many academics, in fact, would argue that the question is irrelevant to their pursuit of knowledge.

A 2013 faculty survey at the University of Michigan at Ann Arbor found that 66% believed that external engagement was complementary to their academic research.[56] Roughly 40%, however, believed it was time-consuming and distracting, and 34% believed public engagement was downright dangerous, mainly due to the risk of being misquoted, or having scholarly work misrepresented, by the media. A Pew Research Center/AAAS survey found similar results: 43% of 3,748 scientists surveyed believe that it is important for scientists to get coverage for their work in the news media, but 79% believe that the news media can't discriminate between well-founded and poorly supported scientific findings.[57] A 2014 study by John Besley in *Science and Public Policy* further showed that many academics do not see their role "as an enabler of direct public participation in decision-making through formats such as deliberative meetings, and do not believe there are personal benefits for investing in these activities."[58]

Yet we all have reason to be concerned about the quality of the public scientific discourse in this country. Scientific information has been used and misused to drive partisan agendas and so-called "culture wars." And the American public does not appear to be a discerning consumer of that information. Consider this disturbing pair of facts: (1) surveys by the California Academy of Sciences and the National Science Foundation show that a majority of the U.S. public is unable to pass even a basic scientific literacy test and does not clearly understand the scientific process, and yet; (2) a survey by the Carsey Institute at the University of New Hampshire found that 83% of respondents reported a "great deal" or "moderate" understanding of climate change issues.[59] While Americans tend to have confidence in their technical and scientific understanding of climate change, data proves otherwise. Scientific illiteracy is driving the social debate over climate change, and that stands in the way of meaningful and informed action.

For this to change, we need a more socially literate scientific community and a more scientifically literate public. Responsibility for the poor state of the public and political debate on a range of scientific issues falls, in part, on the academic community. The challenge we face is about science communication as much as it is about the science itself.

We live in an age when scientific issues permeate our social, economic, and political culture, and people must be educated on science and the scientific process if we are to make rational and informed decisions that affect our future. Indeed, a well-functioning democracy requires it. Yet the relative absence of academics and academic scholarship in the public discourse creates a vacuum into which uninformed, wrong, and downright destructive viewpoints get voiced and take hold.

After the Deepwater Horizon oil spill in the Gulf of Mexico, for example, conservative pundit Rush Limbaugh argued that "The ocean will take care of this on its own if it was left alone and left out there . . . It's natural. It's as natural as the ocean water is."[60] Meanwhile, scientists continue to study the spill's outcomes: major ongoing damage to aquatic ecosystems and chronic health effects on people. But all too often this kind of valuable knowledge is left on the academic table, unable to compete with the tenor and tone of pundits and fails to reach the attention of policy-makers and the public, who need it desperately.

We need another Carl Sagan, someone who can take complex scientific ideas and make them understandable to a lay audience. We need many Carl Sagans, people who can present academic information in a way that recognizes both the scientific models that have been developed and the cultural underpinnings that cause people to accept or reject them. Unfortunately, whenever I suggest this to my colleagues, the reply is derision: Sagan was a hack, a popularizer, and a lightweight. Instead, they fall back on safe bromides about how things are "supposed" to work; the public and politicians should simply accept academic conclusions because the scholars' methods and interests are established within their communities and cannot credibly be questioned by outsiders. It's an arrogant attitude, and one that has contributed to the mess we are in now.

But that attitude cannot stand. The role of the academic scholar in society is in flux today. Social media is "democratizing knowledge," allowing all forms of "research" to enter the public discourse and influence the democratic process. At the same time, state legislatures are cutting funds to higher education and there is a growing distortion of the research agenda by funding sources with specific interests. Against this backdrop, academic researchers can continue to write for specialized journals, but in so doing they become further relegated to the sidelines. To revitalize their fields, they must embark on a new effort at public engagement, embracing, in the words of the Berkeley sociologist and proponent of "public sociology" Michael Burawoy, "the necessity and possibility of moving from interpretation to engagement, from theory to practice, from the academy to its publics."[61]

In this new field of public engagement, an academic's success will be measured not in "bricks" such as citation counts, but by the extent to which scholarly research changes the way people think about the problems we face and their solutions. The actual metrics for the attainment of that success are anyone's guess. But that should not discourage any scholar from seeking their vocation in making an impact beyond the campus walls.

13

Public engagement as a balancing act

Each spring, my professorial colleagues and I perform a common ritual: we fill out our annual activities reports to summarize our research, teaching, and service accomplishments for the year. As we do so, we are keenly aware that the primary metric is really research, and, in particular, research published in top-tier academic journals. Attempts at public or political engagement are overlooked or even discouraged as an "impractical" waste of time.

In the same University of Michigan survey mentioned in the previous chapter, fully 56% of faculty felt that external engagement is not valued by tenure committees.[62] Given that these activities will not register in a promotion review, many ask why someone seeking job security would get involved in them at all. This is an important question to consider when we look to the academic scholar to help us improve the sorry state of scientific discourse in this country. Ultimately, why an academic makes the choice to engage in public or political discourse is a personal decision, motivated by his or her own circumstances, values, and beliefs, and driven by his or her own goals.

Unfortunately, many excellent scientists are poor communicators who lack the skills, time, or inclination to play the role of educator to the general public and our political leaders. Academic scholars are often not trained, nor are they given the proper incentives, to do this kind of work. Others are appropriately cautious, asking questions about how they can do this without losing their standing as objective subject-matter experts. Engagement is fraught with hazards and dangers that should not be taken lightly. An academic scholar could easily step over the line of objective science into advocacy and find that they have done irreparable harm to their career and their ability to persuade. So how and where do scholars find the balance point?

The first step might be to recognize that it certainly is possible to do so, as we know from the rich tradition of public intellectualism in the past. *New York Times* commentator David Brooks captured the nature of today's problem when he was asked on a National Public Radio broadcast if he thought any current scholars might have the same influence as the mid-twentieth-century intellectual Reinhold Niebuhr. Brooks replied, "My favorite period of American social science is the period roughly between '55 and '65. And this was a period when you had a series of public intellectuals who were not lost in academic disciplines, but who are much higher-brow than your average journalist . . . the milieu that created these big daring public intellectuals just isn't there right now."[63]

The fact is that many of today's scientists are indeed lost to the academy. The role of the public intellectual has become an arcane and elusive option for today's academic scholar. Constant immersion in academic seminars and journals to the exclusion of practitioner seminars, meetings, and non-scholarly writing has served to weaken literacy in the languages of the public, economic, and political domains.

What we need are some clear guidelines for engagement for the academic community. This is an idea whose time has come. For example, the National Academies has convened two Sackler Colloquia on "the science of science communication." Some disciplines appear to be turning their attention to these issues in their journals. The Leopold Leadership Fellowship is training scholars to "translate their knowledge to action and for catalyzing change." And organizations like the Union of Concerned Scientists and COMPASS are developing practical guides to help the growing community of scientists who are willing to take the next step in ensuring their research and expertise are making a valuable contribution to society. But these are isolated examples. The underlying institutions of academia must change.

The first place to start this change is the system of formal rewards and tenure. While recognition dinners and other activities can be used to honor faculty for engagement, the formal structures of tenure are the greatest source of resistance and therefore the greatest lever for real change. Altered tenure, review, and promotion criteria will encourage more diversity in a school's faculty portfolio. For example, the Ross School of Business at the University of Michigan has added "practice" as a fourth category to their annual review process with the goal of encouraging faculty to work on problems that have real value to the private sector. Another solution is to allow more flexibility in determining who is a peer or colleague in the review process. A junior faculty member who has performed public or political engagement should be evaluated by peers who have conducted this type of work, as well as those who are more focused on scholarly merit. Ultimately, we must consider the question of whether a faculty member whose engagement outweighs their publication record can be tenured.

But changing the rules of tenure is not easily tackled by schools in isolation. Academia is a competitive market, wherein faculty members act as free agents. If one school establishes idiosyncratic metrics for tenure, an untenured junior faculty member would be taking a chance by pursuing this alternative path. The risk of a resume that is not valued by the broader market is too great.

Beyond such strategic considerations, the question remains of how can we quantify and assess the quality of engagement. The peer review process has been well vetted as a means of evaluating the impact of academic research, but this does not readily translate to the assessment of engagement-based work. For example, it is easier than ever to reach a wide audience, to join and inform discussion, to disseminate knowledge and reach out to communities using the widening array of social media tools. But how does one measure the value of this activity? What is the intellectual value of a blog with one million page views? How does this compare with academic citation counts, which average only 10.41 across all fields between 2000 and 2010 according to Thomson Reuters (that average drops to 4.67 for the social sciences)?[64] How can such metrics be combined to capture an academic's overall impact? One possibility lies in social media analytics, which increasingly can be refined to focus on the impact on selective demographics, providing a means to quantify impact in a way that is as rigorous as peer review.

But the informal faculty culture must also change. Changing metrics and formal reward systems can only take us so far as long as many of us are culturally biased away from engagement.

Here we might look to the increasing number of scholars who quietly deviate from the rules of academia and participate in public engagement. These people are gaining valuable knowledge and experience that can help the rest of the academy learn how to engage effectively while remaining credible within the academy. They can teach us all the new rules of the game. They can show us how engagement can be messy and hostile, but also rewarding and research enhancing.

Public debate plays by a different set of rules than academic debate. Scientists lose control of the message they intended their data and models to convey as competing interests either use, attack, or distort their message to further their own political goals. Beyond the messiness of social debate, it can also be hostile. If you are saying something important, you will receive blowback—as the aphorism states, "If you are not offending anyone, you never took a stand." The hostility doesn't necessarily mean that you are wrong or even that you presented your ideas inappropriately. You just need to be ready to receive engagement in all its forms, ugly and otherwise.

Many scholars receive hate mail. Some of my collection includes: "Scum, You think you are doing good, but you are working for Satan," "You and University of Michigan are criminals," "please by all means, just kill yourself," "Warming terrorists need a spanking. No son of a bitch green terrorist listens to reason," and "Sorry you have such an empty life, but I'm going to bet it gets a lot worse from here. Count on it." Others receive far worse. Texas Tech Atmospheric Scientist and evangelical Christian Katherine Hayhoe began to receive hers after Newt Gingrich publicly dropped her from a book he was editing when he decided to run for President in 2012. Rush Limbaugh subsequently ridiculed her as a "climate babe" and she began receiving messages like "you are nothing but a liar, you lie," "[Misogynistic vulgarism] Nazi Bitch Whore Climatebecile [. . .] You stupid bitch, You are a mass murderer . . ." Kerry Emmanuel, Professor of Atmospheric Science at MIT, and a self-identified Republican, reported receiving an unprecedented "frenzy of hate," threatening him and his wife after he was interviewed by Climate Desk.[65]

Michael Mann, Penn State Climatologist and creator of the famous "hockey stick" graph of increasing global temperatures, describes a barrage of intimidation that includes: an overwhelming number of Freedom of Information Act requests, subpoenas by Republican Congressman Joe Barton, attempts by Ken Cuccinelli, the Republican attorney general of Virginia to have his academic credentials stripped, and being listed in a report by Sen. James Inhofe (R-OK) along with 16 other climate scientists for having engaged in "potentially criminal behavior." On one occasion he was even sent an envelope with powder in it, requiring the involvement of the FBI. Academic engagement is an important but risky business.

But the benefit of engagement for many is a greater sense of meaning and purpose as they witness the broader community benefit from their life's work. On a more practical note, engagement can even improve your research. Engagement and collaboration with the public can create new knowledge. For the academic, it can yield better future research questions, a deeper appreciation for the nuanced context in which that research is done, and an expanded network of partners for exploring that context. For the community, it can empower people to offer input and guidance on research that can have an impact on their lives, inform their own decision-making with regards to political and social issues, demystify the ivory tower of the academy and those who inhabit it, and expand their own networks for seeking assistance with future issues and challenges.

There is much more work to be done to define the rules of the game for public engagement. Where is the boundary between being a scientific content source and a scientific content advocate? What is the role of the academic scientist and what is the role of others (e.g., NGOs) in the scientific information process? How can the linkages between them be structured to protect the integrity of science and develop evidence-based platforms for communicating that content to policy-makers and the public? These and many other questions hold great importance for both a functioning democracy based on sound scientific reasoning and a vibrant academic community whose work helps us to achieve it.

In answering them, I believe that we will come to realize that a satisfying career will be measured more in the impact we have on how people think and act, and less on citation counts and top-tier journal articles. Further, I believe these new measures of success will become more pronounced with the coming generations. This changing reality is, in many ways, merely a return to the notion of the academy as a special and honored place in society—not above it or separate from it, but part of it. Meanwhile, the price of our current, disengaged approach seems higher every day. One of the ultimate ironies about the climate change debate may be that many of the physical and social scientists that could have helped us to understand the problem better and faster turned down such opportunities in order to write a few more arcane scholarly articles to satisfy their tenure committees.

14

The new environmental scholarship

We are in a new era, a new epoch, a new environmental reality—one that demands that we shift the focus and urgency of our research and understanding. Nobel laureate Paul Crutzen and his colleague Eugene Stoermer introduced the concept of the Anthropocene in 2000, arguing that humankind's impact on Earth has been on the scale of an emergent geological era since at least the industrial revolution of the early 1800s, and has become even more acute since "the Great Acceleration" around 1950 onwards. "Human activity has transformed between a third and a half of the land surface of the planet," wrote Crutzen in a *Nature* commentary. "Many of the world's major rivers have been dammed or diverted; fertilizer plants produce more nitrogen than is fixed naturally by all terrestrial ecosystems; humans use more than half of the world's readily accessible freshwater runoff."[66]

A group of geophysicists led by Johan Rockström of the Stockholm Resilience Centre have sought to define the issue more clearly by identifying key biotic and geochemical markers or "planetary boundaries" beyond which the stability of the planetary-scale systems on which humanity depends cannot be relied upon. Nine have been isolated: climate change, ocean acidification, ozone depletion, atmospheric aerosol loading, phosphorus and nitrogen cycles, global freshwater use, land system change, loss of biodiversity, and chemical pollution. Some scientists believe that three have already been exceeded: climate change, biodiversity loss, and the nitrogen cycle.[67]

While many scientists agree that the idea of the Anthropocene is compelling, it has not yet been accepted and recognized by either geophysical societies or the Academy of Sciences. Formal acknowledgement of an unprecedented shift in our geophysical reality would be a significant event, to say the least. It could inspire us to reduce that impact through changes in behavior and technology; it could also lead us to increase our impact through deliberate "geo-engineering," for example through attempts to manipulate the climate through carbon sequestration and "scrubbing" technologies to remove carbon from the atmosphere.

The Anthropocene era brings considerations for sustainability into a new orientation, one that moves beyond the idea that we must adjust social systems to the limits set by the biosphere, and instead recognizes that we have already surpassed at least some of those limits. The resultant changes in weather, sea level, water availability, and crop yields are all emergent markers of the Anthropocene that point to a fundamental system failure created by our social institutions (most notably the market). We now have control over the biosphere and, therefore, the human systems that depend on it, in ways that are monumental.

The Anthropocene era will demand a new and as yet undefined social order that we might call the Anthropocene Society. The tensions that will accompany such a shift are already playing out in the polarized debate over climate change, which represents one of the planetary boundaries that we have crossed. Many people clearly have trouble believing that human beings are capable of altering natural systems as vast and complex as the global climate; others see the only solution in further manipulation of the climate; still others insist that we downscale our production of greenhouse gases to a point that is once again below the threshold of what the planetary biosphere can absorb. We have only just begun the process of developing a new social–environmental relationship for the Anthropocene. Clive Hamilton, a professor of ethics at Australia's Centre for Applied Philosophy and Public Ethics, has argued that there are no "good" possibilities for Anthropocene Society, only more or less bad. Others are equally pessimistic. "The past half-century has been marked by an exponential explosion of environmental knowledge, technology, regulation, education, awareness, and organizations. But none of this has served to diminish the flow of terrifying scientific warnings about the fate of the planet," wrote Tom Gladwin in the *Oxford Handbook of Business and the Natural Environment*.[68]

The notion of the Anthropocene is an articulation of the disconnect between problem recognition and positive response. It also exposes a paradox in the current research approach within environmental scholarship: we need to both fit the phenomena we are observing within existing theory (in order to contribute to the field and maintain legitimacy within the academy through publication, promotion, and tenure), and step outside of existing theory to fully capture the magnitude and scope of the problems. We have become comfortable with the first of these two approaches; within the academy, it is polite, acceptable, and unchallenging to address how we might mitigate the impact we are having on the environment. To take the second step, we will need to reenergize and re-radicalize the field, returning to the tone of the early environmental movement, when scholars of environmental issues resided outside of mainstream scholarship and practice in order to criticize and challenge the underlying institutions of the field. The Anthropocene era calls for scholars to do that again, to enter a realm of creative destruction that questions taken-for-granted metrics and assumptions, to be impolite and unacceptable, to challenge existing power structures.

What we need now is a correction in academic research and education, not only in the physical sciences, but also the social sciences, and not only in discipline-based schools but also professional schools. Business schools should be front and center in such innovation. An outdated and insufficient notion of sustainability has gone mainstream in both the market and in business schools, and researchers and educators in the field are still ill prepared to recognize the full import of the Anthropocene. As Harvard organizational theorist Rakesh Khurana points out in his book *From Higher Aims to Hired Hands*, a business school education has become irrelevant to contemporary challenges like poverty, climate change, species extinction, and social justice in a globalized world.[69]

To keep pace, business education must confront some deep-seated and unquestioned assumptions: the traditional consumption model, belief in constant economic growth, the perverse signals created by discount rates, the short-term thinking promoted by quarterly corporate financial reports, nature having value only as an immediate commodity or feedstock for industrial supply chains, etc. MBA programs will need to balance cool new apps and the latest in consulting techniques with a renewed commitment to cultivating change agents who can lead their companies from within to meet the tremendous challenges we face as a society.

The Anthropocene business school must amend the dominant theories and models, such as agency theory and investor capitalism, rather than comfortably rest within them. It must consider the role of humans within the context of the natural environment, not independent from it. Models of management must expand from a focus on individual components and divisions to recognize the entire system and its interconnections. Models of governance must break down siloed and defensive mentalities and push toward radical transparency.

A truly sustainable energy system, for example, cannot be conceived of as a single wind farm or solar array—it must include the whole of generation, transmission, distribution, demand management, and, importantly, mobility. Models of operations must consider closed-loop models bound by finite resources and place a value on natural capital, in part by pricing negative externalities properly. A growing emphasis will need to be placed on more local as opposed to global options for material delivery, with implications for accounting, finance, and organizational design. Models of strategy must move beyond stale forms of winner-take-all competition to consider cross-sector collaboration that improves the state of the entire economy and the society it is designed to serve.

Overall, business education that brings us toward a more sustainable world recognizes that, collectively, human ideas are an infinite resource and human hope and ingenuity can overcome our sustainability challenges. Yet tomorrow's leaders will not simply be standard-bearers for the models of capitalism that brought us through the twentieth century. Instead, we need to encourage what Stanford professor of education Deb Meyerson calls "tempered radicals": people who are able to understand and work within existing systems, but are also cognizant of competing models that attend to the new challenges of the twenty-first century.[70] Indeed, this mindset might well be the one that we all need at this, the dawn of the Anthropocene Society.

IV
Changing Culture and Values

15 Culture and carbon

We place too much faith in pricing as a singular mechanism for solving environmental problems in this country. The most vivid example is the call to set a price for carbon as the means to address climate change. As the logic goes, if we set a high enough price for carbon, innovators will swiftly invent gadgets that emit fewer greenhouse gases than today's products, investors will invest in them, companies will manufacture them, and consumers will buy them.

Not so fast. People don't behave like mice chasing a piece of cheese whenever it is placed in front of them. We are not so singular in focus. We actually care who is placing the cheese, and may even ignore the cheese if it is not placed in the right way. Pricing is never contextually or politically inert. Contrary to what many would like to think, a price for carbon is not an all-embracing quick fix, but one tool that must be accompanied by others in order to make sure that markets respond effectively and efficiently. Put too much faith in pricing as the only answer and success will be either elusive or found through sheer luck.

Consider the gasoline price spike in 2007. The market responded: sales of gas-guzzling vehicles dropped like a stone and consumers flocked to fuel-efficient options. Pricing worked! But consider an alternative scenario. Imagine we faced the same gasoline price spike, but instead of its cause being the invisible hand of the market, it was the very visible hand of a government gas tax. Would consumers have been so pliable? Would auto suppliers have been so flummoxed? No. Unlike our friends in Europe, who have accepted government-inflated gasoline prices, it is likely that here in the U.S. such an act would have triggered a widespread revolt of defiant customers and intractable auto executives.

Consider one more example. In 2002, the Irish government instituted a 15 cent fee (aka tax) on plastic grocery bags. Within one year, plastic grocery bag use dropped by 94%. Score one for pricing-induced behavior change! Well, not entirely. Unlike in San Francisco and many other U.S. cities, where attempts to institute similar initiatives have become flashpoints of social conflict, the context in Ireland was ripe for the "plastax."

The reasons, in no particular order, include the fact that there were no plastic bag manufacturers in Ireland to mount an organized opposition; there was no problem of "leakage" to neighboring jurisdictions where the tax would not be levied; almost all of Ireland's grocery stores had computerized cash registers that had already been programmed to collect a national sales tax, making it easy to implement the bag tax; and the country has a young, flexible population that has proved to be a good testing ground for innovation in other cases, from the adoption of cellphone services to the acceptance of non-smoking laws.

What's more, the country was primed for change, having just shifted their currency from the Irish pound (aka the punt) to the euro, and people generally didn't mind paying the tax, as the litter from plastic bags was seen as a common nuisance. Once the bag tax was put in place in Ireland, it quickly became socially unacceptable to be seen carrying a plastic bag. In fact, it was considered downright rude, with violators being treated in much the same way as people who do not curb their dogs.

The lesson of Ireland's plastax is that markets respond to pricing—sometimes. The management consulting multinational McKinsey & Company has developed a well-known analysis called a "cost abatement curve" for reducing greenhouse-gas emissions. The curve shows that many greenhouse-gas-reducing technologies are already cost-effective today. Most of these technologies are within the construction industry: insulation, lighting, water heating, etc. Yet many of these technologies remain largely unadopted. Why?

It comes down to cultural context. Of all industries, construction is one of the slowest to change. Despite tremendous advances stimulated by the U.S. Green Building Council, inertia typically rules the day, particularly in the small and fragmented home-building sector. From my years as a general contractor, I know that home-builders can be extremely risk-averse. And even if a contractor decided to take the risk of installing something new and unfamiliar (such as graywater-recycling systems), he or she would face the risk of banks refusing to loan money to support "unproven" technology, building inspectors balking at that technology's novelty, or the customer requesting a callback if it doesn't work as advertised.

That assumes that the customer knows enough to want and trust the new technology. The appliance manufacturer Whirlpool once considered taking the Energy Star label off its washers because consumers thought that if the machines used less water and less energy, they must also clean clothes less well. The company still finds consumers who balk at buying the super-efficient washers at as much as a $700 price premium—even though an average family of four can get that money back in water and energy savings in less than two years in some parts of the country.

These sorts of barriers to the shift to more sustainable products and policies are not uncommon. After all, we are talking about human behavior here. And while pricing is one factor in driving that behavior, individual psychology and social norms also play an enormous role, and are often overlooked—they are just too messy and too hard to consider. By comparison, pricing models seem relatively straightforward.

But as the public and politicians consider how to create the proper price for carbon, they must consider other instruments for breaking down the inertia of the market. For example, the government can stimulate markets through its tremendous purchasing power (the Clinton administration was instrumental in jump-starting the paper recycling industry by mandating that government agencies buy recycled paper). It can also stimulate innovation through its research and development labs. It can mandate change through Renewable Portfolio Standards (policies that require utilities to source a specified percentage of their energy from renewable sources). It can make me or the farmer down the road into energy entrepreneurs by establishing Net Metering (which allows home owners to sell excess energy from their home solar array back to the utility) or Feed-In-Tarriffs (which allow commercial landowners to install large-scale wind or solar power sources and enter into long-term purchasing contracts with utilities). And it can make the future market for innovation more predictable by stabilizing the Production Tax Credit over an extended period of time.

Economics can get us started on the path of shifting markets, but behavioral and social sciences such as psychology, sociology, and business management can help us understand the inherent humanness of markets. President Obama understood that his challenge in averting a more severe collapse during the Great Recession was as much psychological and sociological as it was economic. So, too, is the challenge we face over climate change—and the stakes are higher still.

16

Culture and climate

In January 2014, the eastern and southern United States were plunged into extraordinarily frigid temperatures that stranded air travelers, stressed power grids, closed schools, and killed more than 20 people. In all, the lives of more than 187 million people (roughly 60% of Americans) were affected by the record-breaking cold. Meteorologists identified the "polar vortex" as the culprit: a large cyclone, first studied in 1853, which gyres around the North Pole. Much to these scientists' dismay, they then watched their explanation become yet another flashpoint in the rhetorical war over climate change.

On the one side, Rush Limbaugh called the polar vortex an invention of the liberal left to further promote the global-warming agenda.[71] *Fox News* referred to it as the "so-called" polar vortex, and aired multiple pundits claiming that global warming cannot be real because the winter was so cold.[72] Under a regular blog called "Planet Gore" (named for former vice president and climate activist Al Gore), the *National Review* made the mocking declaration that "there is absolutely nothing that 'global warming' can't be linked to if you try hard enough."[73] Then a Russian research vessel became stranded in the Arctic while studying, among other things, global warming. That led Donald Trump to enter the fray with a tweet:

> This very expensive GLOBAL WARMING bullshit has got to stop. Our planet is freezing, record low temps, and our GW scientists are stuck in ice.

On the other side, a headline in *Climate Central* pronounced that the "Polar vortex in U.S. may be example of global warming." A *Time* magazine headline concurred that "Climate change might just be driving the historic cold snap," adding that "melting Arctic ice is making sudden cold snaps more likely—not less." *Common Dreams* went even further, arguing that "every weather event in the modern world is attributable to climate change." A great deal of effort also turned toward attacking the contrarian viewpoint. *The Weather Channel*, for example, ran a story headlined "Polar vortex and climate change: Why Rush Limbaugh and others are wrong."

This is what stands for public debate today. Climate change has been transformed into a rhetorical contest more akin to the spectacle of a sports match, pitting one side against the other with the goal of victory through the cynical use of politics, fear, distrust, and intolerance. No wonder the public is confused. But why did an issue like climate change become so toxic? When nearly 200 scientific agencies around the world (including the most prestigious in every one of the G8 countries) and 97% of peer-reviewed journal articles between 1991 and 2011 endorse the position that human-influenced climate change is happening, why is there such an emotional and vitriolic debate over this single scientific issue?

The American debate over climate change turns on two main themes. One is the science of the problem; the other is government measures, or the lack thereof, to fix it. Many believe these themes cover the entire debate. They're wrong—at its root, it is a debate over culture, values, ideology, and worldviews.

Climate change has been enmeshed in the culture wars, where beliefs about science often align with beliefs about abortion, gun control, health care, evolution, or other issues that fall along the contemporary political divide. This was not the case even as recently as the 1990s, and it is not the case in Europe. This is a distinctly American phenomenon.

Several years ago, I analyzed the ways that climate skeptics framed the issue both at a major conference and in U.S. newspaper editorials from 2007 to 2009. What emerged was a set of cultural themes that reflect the deeper ideological undercurrents of this debate.

For skeptics, climate change is inextricably tied to a belief that climate science and policy are a covert way for liberal environmentalists and the government to diminish citizens' personal freedom. Other prominent themes include a strong faith in the free market, an overriding fear that climate legislation will hinder economic progress, and a suspicion that green jobs and renewable energy are ploys for government to engineer (and therefore destroy) the market.

The most intriguing of the skeptics' traits is a powerful distrust of the scientific peer-review process, and of scientists themselves. "Peer review," to a climate skeptic's eye, is really "pal review," in which establishment scientist-editors only publish work by those whose research findings agree with their own. Scientists themselves are seen as intellectual elites, studying issues that are beyond the reach of the ordinary person's scrutiny. Physical scientists, such as geologists, ecologists, and climatologists, are mystified and frustrated by this state of affairs. Given the level of vitriol, who can blame them? I, and many of my colleagues, are regular recipients of climate-skeptic hate mail and a few have received far worse.

But social scientists from the fields of psychology, sociology, anthropology, political science, ethics, and philosophy try to make sense of such powerful and contradictory reactions to the issue of climate change. These disciplines offer valuable tools for both understanding why people take such polarized views on controversial issues and sorting out how to move beyond the rancor.

Social scientists view the public's variable understanding of climate change not as the result of a lack of adequate information, but as the intentional and unintentional avoidance of that information. That avoidance is rooted in our culture and psychology, and can be summarized in four central points.

First, we all use cognitive filters. When it comes to climate change, physical scientists simply do not hold the final word in public debate. Instead, the public filters statements from the scientific community through their own worldviews. Applying what is called "motivated reasoning," most of us relate to climate change through our prior ideological preferences, personal experiences, and knowledge. We search for information and reach conclusions about highly complex and politically contested issues in a way that will lead us to find supportive evidence of our pre-existing beliefs.

Second, our cognitive filters reflect our cultural identity. We tend to develop worldviews that are consistent with the values held by others within the groups with which we self-identify. Yale University law and psychology professor Dan Kahan calls this "cultural cognition"; we are influenced by group values and will generally endorse positions that most directly reinforce the connections we have with others in our social groups.[74] It is not necessarily that we reject scientific conclusions in this process, but that they are weighted and valued differently depending on how our friends, colleagues, trusted sources, or respected leaders frame these issues. We are the product of our surroundings, both chosen and unchosen.

Third, our cultural identity can overpower scientific reasoning. For example, research has found that when belief or disbelief in climate change becomes connected to our cultural identity, being confronted with contrary scientific evidence can actually make us more resolute in resisting conclusions that are at variance with our own. Sociologists Aaron McCright from Michigan State University and Riley Dunlap from Oklahoma State University found that increased education about and self-reported understanding of climate science corresponds with greater concern about climate change among those who already believe in it, and less concern among those who do not.[75] Similarly, Kahan and his colleagues have found that "members of the public with the highest degrees of science literacy and technical reasoning capacity . . . were the ones among whom cultural polarization was greatest."[76] In short, increased knowledge about climate science tends to strengthen our position on climate change—regardless of what that position is. This conclusion is a direct challenge to the common assumption that more scientific information will help convince Americans of the need to deal with climate change. Instead, the key to engaging the debate is addressing the deeper ideological, cultural, and social filters that are triggered by this issue.

Fourth, our political economy generates inertia when it comes to climate action. We cannot discuss the social processes that guide our thinking without also considering the economic, political, and technological reality that is the enactment of our values. We live our lives within a vast physical infrastructure based to a large degree on the use of fossil fuels, and we understand, whether consciously or unconsciously, that this lifestyle cannot be replaced easily. Within this entrenched system, meanwhile, strong economic and political interests are threatened by the issue of climate change; many of them have adopted strategies to confuse and polarize the debate in order to protect their interests. Efforts to change our cultural views on climate change must include efforts to change the institutions of our economy and be prepared to deal with resistance from those who currently benefit from them.

All of these processes can be seen playing out in the United States at the present time, where the opposing cultural worldviews on climate change map onto our partisan political system—a 2013 survey by the Pew Research Center found that only 46% of Republicans believed that "there is solid evidence the earth is warming," while the corresponding number for Democrats was 84%.[77] With the battles lines drawn, the social debate around climate change devolves into a cultural schism.

A similar rift emerged years earlier in the abortion debate, where each side now debates different issues (life versus choice), creates information systems that consistently reinforce their position and disconfirm the other's, and demonizes those who disagree with them. Over time, these positions become increasingly rigid and exclusive, thickening boundaries between cultural communities. Extreme positions ultimately dominate the conversation, the potential for discussion or resolution disintegrates, and the issue becomes stalemated and intractable.

Will this happen in the climate change debate? I am optimistic that it won't, but it is not inconceivable. In the end, the polar vortex has become a part of the lexicon of our society, in much the same way that El Niño has. This can give us hope that we can move beyond the acrimony that has marked the climate debate and finally accept the assessments of the scientific community for what they offer: data-based, theory-driven models and measures for understanding the complexity of the natural environment. While an acceptance of such models often challenges our beliefs and values, this society has built much of its infrastructure and lifestyle on science, and we have shown many times in the past that we can change our worldviews as science reveals new understandings. I, for one, believe there is such a thing as an atom; that it has a nucleus with electrons flying around it; that my body is made up of billions of these things. I have never seen them; I certainly cannot prove they exist. But I trust that they do, because I trust the institutions of science. In the case of climate change, we must once again let that trust overrule our cultural biases.

17

Detoxifying the climate change debate

In 2015, California Governor Jerry Brown described Senator Ted Cruz as unfit to run for president of the United States because of his "direct falsification of the existing scientific data" on climate change.[78] Cruz fired back that "global warming alarmists" like Brown "ridicule and insult anyone who actually looks at the real data."[79] Here we go again. This is one more example of the toxicity of the public debate over climate change.

To detoxify the debate, we need to understand the social forces at work. To those who disbelieve in climate change, the issue amounts to a hoax, humans have no significant impact on the climate, and nothing unusual is happening. To those who do believe, we are in the midst of an imminent crisis, human activity explains all current climate changes, and this will devastate life on Earth as we know it. Amidst this acrimonious din, scientists are trying to explain the complexity of the issue.

To reach some form of social consensus on this issue, we have to disengage from fixed battles on the scientific front and instead seek approaches that engage people who are undecided about climate change on multiple social and cultural fronts.

To begin, we have to stop focusing a disproportionate amount of attention on the people at the extreme poles of the debate, those who are distorting the science and engaging in a contest that they are simply trying to "win." Those of us who believe that climate change is a real and pressing crisis must focus less on the small minority of active deniers and more on the vulnerability of the majority to their influence. In the words of Anthony Leiserowitz, director of the Yale Project on Climate Change Communication, "The proper model for thinking about the climate debate is not a boxing match, but a jury trial. We can never convince the die-hard skeptics, just like a prosecutor will never convince the defense lawyer, and doesn't try. Rather, we should focus on convincing the silent jury of the mass public."[80]

When analyzing highly complex or politically contested scientific concepts about which we have a limited understanding, our reasoning is suffused with emotion. *Washington Post* energy and environment reporter Chris Mooney writes:

> Our positive and negative feelings about people, things, and ideas arise much more rapidly than our conscious thoughts, in a matter of milliseconds . . . We're not driven only by emotions, of course—we also reason, deliberate. But reasoning comes later, works slower.[81]

And as New York University social psychologist Jonathan Haidt points out:

> We may think we are acting as scientists when analyzing data and models, but very often we are acting more as lawyers, using our reasoning to a predetermined end, one that was emotionally biased by our ideological positions and cultural views.[82]

Here are two tactics we might use, then, for reaching the undecided middle and those climate skeptics who ask critical questions (as differentiated from disbelievers engaged in a close-minded campaign to debunk the science). First, we should acknowledge that climate change is a complex issue that is embedded in many social and political concerns. The second tactic is to recognize that there are many more avenues to address concern over climate change than a focus on climate science itself.

For example, Pope Francis speaks about climate change as an issue of faith and social equity: the world's poor will be hit first and hardest even though they did little to contribute to the problem. The Center for Naval Analyses Military Advisory Board, a group of eleven retired three- and four-star military officers, sees it as an issue of national security, a "threat multiplier" and "catalyst for conflict" that will destabilize vulnerable regions of the world and require military deployment.[83]

Meanwhile, the *Lancet*, one of the leading medical journals in the world, considers climate change a health issue, posing a risk to vulnerable populations around the globe. Influential *New York Times* columnist Thomas Friedman warns that climate change is an issue of economic competitiveness—if the United States does not stimulate innovation in the next generation of renewable energy technologies, we will be forced to buy them from nations like China and Germany. Swiss Re, a leading global reinsurance company, positions the issue as one of insurance coverage in the face of natural catastrophes, business interruption, and corporate director and officer liabilities—and so the firm considers climate change in these policies to protect against such liabilities. Jay Gulledge at the Center for Climate and Energy Solutions has framed the issue as one of risk management: in much the same way that one buys home insurance for the low-probability but high-consequence risk of a house fire, we as a society should protect against the low-probability/high-consequence profile of climate change through investments in technology and behavior change. Management consulting firm McKinsey & Company, meanwhile, presents the issue as a market shift, one that will require companies to develop climate change mitigation and adaptation strategies to succeed.

Each of these approaches is founded on the assumption either that climate change is a real problem or has a substantial probability of being a real problem. Each is a different way of framing the issue, and each of the representatives who frame it has the potential to reach populations that the current leading voices on climate action—scientists, environmentalists, and Democratic politicians—cannot. People are more likely to consider evidence when it is accepted or, ideally, presented by a knowledgeable member of their cultural community.

So how you present climate change is as important as what information you present. In America, citing either *Fox News* or Al Gore will draw a fundamentally different emotional response. Each represents not only different positions on climate change, but different belief systems and worldviews. When speaking to a conservative, invoke a conservative; when speaking to an evangelical, invoke an evangelical. Given that many Republicans do not believe there is solid evidence of global warming, the most effective "climate broker" would best come from the political right.

Only by broadening the scope of the debate to embrace this social and cultural complexity can we ever hope to achieve broad-scale public consensus. More scientific data can only take us so far; engaging the inherently human aspects of this debate will take us the rest of the way.

V
A Call to a Calling

18

Pope Francis as messenger

I earlier recalled the words of conservationist Aldo Leopold, who wrote in 1949 that only an "internal change in our intellectual emphasis, loyalties, affections, and convictions" could transform our ethical appreciation of nature. He followed that line with this one: "The proof that conservation has not yet touched these foundations of conduct lies in the fact that philosophy and religion have not yet heard of it."[84]

In the summer of 2015, Pope Francis released his encyclical letter *Laudato Si'*, or *On Care for Our Common Home.*[85] Never before has an encyclical letter received such attention, much less been such a sensation, as to be leaked in advance by the media. His message hit a sensitive spot in the public and political psyche. Aldo Leopold would be pleased.

Scholars, critics, and pundits will analyze and assess Pope Francis's words for years to come. But one aspect of the encyclical letter becomes clear to anyone who reads it: it is impressively expansive, covering environmental science, economics, international politics, carbon credits, social equity, technology, consumerism, social media, theology, and much more. Getting to the root of our ecological crisis, the pope calls on us to "promote a new way of thinking about human beings, life, society, and our relationship with nature."

In many ways, *Laudato Si'* is a call to a calling—a bold appeal to reevaluate our worldviews, values, and spiritual beliefs in light of the urgent environmental challenges of our times. In that sense, it resonates with and reflects my own vocation in this book, and threads together many of the themes I've addressed. Whether you are Catholic or not, religious or secular, there is merit in a closer look at this thought-provoking letter to humanity.

The pope's statement will have a profound impact on the public debate around sustainability. It has elevated the spiritual, moral, and religious dimensions of the issue, asking that people protect the global climate because it is sacred, both for its own God-given value and for its vital importance to the life and dignity of all humankind.

Making a case for sustainability on theological grounds builds on long-standing arguments in the Catholic catechism that environmental degradation is a violation of the seventh commandment, "Thou shalt not steal," as it involves theft from future generations and the poor. Against such a moral backdrop, the more familiar argument that we must focus first and foremost on the business case to protect the global climate seems selfish, shortsighted, and rather absurd.

But perhaps even more important than the content of the message is the messenger. The pope can reach segments of the population that the three primary messengers on climate change—environmentalists, Democratic politicians, and scientists—cannot. One of the problems in communicating about climate change is that it has been ghettoized as a strictly environmental issue promoted by liberal messengers. This makes it easy for some to dismiss it. But the pope can change that.

First, the pope can reach the world's 1.2 billion Roman Catholics with an unmatched capacity to convince and motivate. Religion, unlike any other institutional force in society, has the power to directly influence our values and beliefs. By connecting climate change to spiritual and religious values, and introducing notions of sin, the pope's encyclical will give people new and more powerful motivations to act. Once his message is out, Catholics will hear it reinforced in homilies in their home parish. The pope can make the issue as personal as Sunday school.

And it would appear that Catholics are a receptive audience. According to a 2014 survey by the Yale Project on Climate Communication, a solid majority of Catholics (70%) in the U.S. think that global warming is happening and 48% think it is caused by humans, compared with only 57% and 35% of non-Catholic Christians respectively.[86]

The pope has added the religious voice and authority of the Catholic Church to a growing social movement to recognize and respond to climate change. But the pope's reach extends far beyond his Catholic followers. A 2014 survey by the Pew Research Center found that the pope is extremely popular with both Catholics and non-Catholics. Americans are particularly fond of Pope Francis, with more than three-quarters (78%) giving him positive marks. Though that number dipped to 55% (and 68% of American Catholics) in the months immediately after his largely left-leaning speech to the U.S. Congress and the United Nations in the fall 2015, his popularity remains strong. In Europe, Catholics and non-Catholics view the pope with similar admiration.

Laudato Si' has also drawn attention to the ongoing efforts to address climate change by leaders in other denominations, among them Ecumenical Patriarch Bartholomew I of the Orthodox Church, nicknamed the "Green Patriarch." The Dalai Lama endorsed the letter shortly after its release, and later joined 14 other senior Buddhists in issuing a call for a complete and rapid phase-out of fossil fuels. The Islamic Foundation for Ecology and Environmental Sciences has issued a Muslim declaration on climate change that mirrors many of the themes contained in the pope's encyclical.

This addition to the public debate sets the stage for potential change within our political system. At the time of the encyclical letter's release, the U.S. Congress had 138 Catholic Congressman (70 of whom were Republicans) and 26 Catholic Senators (11 of whom are Republicans). Those 81 Republicans have rejected the scientific consensus on climate change, not only because of their personal views on the topic, but also often to yield to party politics.

In the end, the best possible outcome of the pope's message for Americans would be to encourage the breakdown of the partisan divide over climate change and the reestablishment of societal trust in our scientific institutions.

On the one side, Democrats may learn a powerful lesson about the need to go beyond the scientific arguments on the issue and begin to connect it to people's underlying values, which could help motivate action across the political spectrum.

On the other, the pope's message could give additional political cover for Republicans to upend the notion that you can't be a conservative and believe in climate change, or, in the more extreme case, that you can't believe in God and believe in climate change (as Rush Limbaugh and many others have argued).

Early in 2015, 50 Senators, including 15 Republicans, voted for an amendment that affirmed that humans contribute to global warming. In September 2015, 11 House Republicans signed a resolution that recognized humans have a role in causing climate change and endorsed steps to address it. Other Republicans, too, have begun to chip away at what former Utah governor Jon Huntsman called the party's "anti-science" position. This past March, for example, Republican Senator Lindsey Graham from South Carolina blamed his party—well, and Al Gore—for the stalemate over climate change and concluded:

> You know, when it comes to climate change being real, people of my party are all over the board . . . I think the Republican Party has to do some soul searching. Before we can be bipartisan, we've got to figure out where we are as a party . . . What is the environmental platform of the Republican Party? I don't know, either.[87]

Some will surely undertake this conversion as a personal reexamination of their beliefs or in response to the shifting values of a reenergized base. This may be especially true for those with a faith-based dimension to their platform—opposing the pope on the grounds that they segregate their religious selves from their political selves will ring hollow with much of the electorate to whom they are trying to appeal.

A 2015 poll found that two-thirds of Americans were more likely to vote for political candidates who campaign on fighting climate change (including 48% of Republicans) and less likely to vote for candidates who deny climate science.[88] The truth is that many Republican politicians, congressional aides, lobbyists, and staff will admit, when safely behind closed doors, that they believe climate change is happening and has human causes. Don't believe it? A 2015 survey found that 54% of self-described conservative Republicans had come to believe that the world's climate is changing and that humankind plays some role in the change, up from just 35% in 2009.[89] The party is beginning to roll on this issue, and better late than not at all. Nonetheless, a 2014 Gallup poll still found that climate change and the quality of the environment ranked near the bottom of concerns among Republicans.[90]

Pope Francis's encyclical letter calls on people to be more engaged in political life: "Love, overflowing with small gestures of mutual care, is also civic and political, and it makes itself felt in every action that seeks to build a better world." His message appears specifically concerned with a compelling new approach to the determination of the "common good," presenting virtuous civic and political behavior as being not only about relationships between individuals, but also "macro-relationships, social, economic, and political ones."

This is the ultimate importance of the pope's encyclical: it compels action based on deeply held beliefs that go to the core of who we are. Once these beliefs are embedded, no cost–benefit analysis, no false dichotomy of jobs versus the environment, is at play. When delivered from the church, synagogue, mosque, or temple and connected to millennia of religious beliefs and traditions, the message of climate change will be internalized to a degree far greater than any government policy or economic incentive could ever achieve. The stage will be set for business and political leaders to step forward and take action. Without such deep conviction, it is quite possible that action will forever fall short of the challenge.

19

To till and keep the garden

In 1967, the historian Lynn White wrote that our ecological problems derive from "Christian attitudes towards man's relation to nature," which lead us to think of ourselves as "superior to nature, contemptuous of it, willing to use it for our slightest whim."[91] He doubted that changes in those attitudes could occur unless, first, "orthodox Christian arrogance towards nature" were somehow dispelled and, secondly, we move beyond that idea that science and technology alone can solve our ecological crisis.

With *Laudato Si'*, Pope Francis is calling us to dispel that arrogance. And, where Lynn White's essay caused an uproar of resistance, resentment, and controversy, the pope's message must inevitably do the same. No "internal change in our intellectual emphasis, loyalties, affections, and convictions" can occur without some discomfort and pain.

Indeed, if it did not, it could not possibly address the root causes of our environmental problems to the fullest extent.

Francis blames rampant consumerism, unrestrained faith in technology, blind pursuit of profits, political shortsightedness, and the economic inequalities that force the world's poor to bear the brunt of an imbalanced system. We live in a world where the richest 20% of the world's population (namely us) consumes 86% of all goods and services, while the poorest 20% consumes just 1.3%. Indeed, income inequality is growing to extreme proportions. In the U.S., the gap between rich and poor is the highest it has been since 1928.[92] It is not a giant leap to connect these injustices with a call to act on climate change to fulfill and enact our religious beliefs.

Pope Francis calls for a reexamination of the Judeo-Christian idea that the "stewardship" written about within the book of Genesis grants us dominion over nature. He writes that this "is not a correct interpretation of the Bible as understood by the Church."

Instead, he writes, the Bible teaches human beings to "till and keep" the garden that is our world, where *tilling* refers to cultivating, plowing, or working, while *keeping* means caring, protecting, overseeing, and preserving. We are called on to do both: our work must still care for the land and waters. At a more personal level, the pope's encyclical asks people to "realize that their responsibility within creation, and their duty towards nature and the Creator, are an essential part of their faith," and that "an awareness of the gravity of today's cultural and ecological crisis must be translated into new habits." These are profound and unsettling challenges and, for the business sector, they could manifest in changes in consumer and investor behavior.

"Purchasing is always a moral—and not simply economic—act," Pope Francis writes. It is notoriously difficult to inspire shifts in behavior, especially habitual behavior, but the pope goes far beyond general spiritual arguments to be quite direct in his prescriptive suggestions. Above all else, the encyclical letter promotes individual virtue in consuming less:

> A person who could afford to spend and consume more but regularly uses less heating and wears warmer clothes, shows the kind of convictions and attitudes which help to protect the environment. There is a nobility in the duty to care for creation through little daily actions.

The question for executives is whether the pope's message, along with similar statements from other spiritual leaders, will begin to compel consumers and the businesses, institutions, and organizations they are a part of to change their purchasing habits, for example to buy more fuel-efficient cars, appliances, homes, and other products (or not to buy them at all) as a matter of religious duty. Not to stop there, the pope calls on us to reject what he terms our current "collective selfishness" in favor of a strong sense of collective responsibility, which could begin a social transformation in our lifestyles at the grassroots level of households and neighborhoods.

Further still, the pope advocates that people use their consuming and purchasing power to shift markets.

> A change in lifestyle could bring healthy pressure to bear on those who wield political, economic, and social power. This is what consumer movements accomplish by boycotting certain products. They prove successful in changing the way businesses operate, forcing them to consider their environmental footprint and their patterns of production. When social pressure affects their earnings, businesses clearly have to find ways to produce differently. This shows us the great need for a sense of social responsibility on the part of consumers.

The encyclical and similar spiritual tracts may even change the behavior of financial investors. The pope's call to believers to "better recognize the ecological commitments which stem from our convictions" will compel some to pay more thoughtful and targeted attention to the fossil-fuel components of their financial portfolios. Large Catholic organizations (such as universities, hospitals, and religious orders) will likely reexamine the question of divestment from the fossil-fuel sector. Certainly, constituents of these organizations, especially students, are petitioning these institutions to act. And some are responding. In 2015, Georgetown University followed the University of Dayton's lead and passed a resolution to divest from "companies whose principal business is mining coal for use in energy production." Might we soon witness a growing financial services sector catering to such investors that wish to heed a spiritual and moral call in all of their actions as consumers?

The pope is adding his weight to that of the increasing number of corporations that view the question of climate policy as an issue of "when," not "if." A 2013 survey of business executives by *MIT Sloan Management Review* and the Boston Consulting Group found that 85% believed that human-induced climate change is real. In 2014, Royal Dutch Shell and Unilever NV joined 68 other companies to urge world governments to cap cumulative carbon emissions and contain rising temperatures. In 2015, the White House launched the American Business Act on Climate pledge, which included 13 of the largest companies in America, including Alcoa, Apple, Bank of America, Berkshire Hathaway Energy, Cargill, Coca-Cola, General Motors, Goldman Sachs, Google, Microsoft, PepsiCo, UPS, and Walmart. There is growing political, social, and now moral momentum to commit to climate action, and to deliver on those commitments. Will the pressures for change overcome the pressures for stasis? As the pope writes:

> Environmental protection cannot be assured solely on the basis of financial calculations of costs and benefits. The environment is one of those goods that cannot be adequately safeguarded or promoted by market forces. Once more, we need to reject a magical conception of the market, which would suggest that problems can be solved simply by an increase in the profits of companies or individuals.

Pope Francis challenges us to turn our minds, hearts, and actions toward nature and respect the value God created in it. Given our relatively new-found ability to alter the environment in globally catastrophic ways, it is important that the world's many people of faith find a call to protect nature for a reason greater and higher than personal self-interest—namely, that God wants and expects us to do so. That has the power to motivate a transformation of our world in ways that are urgently needed.

"Human beings, while capable of the worst, are also capable of rising above themselves, choosing again what is good, and making a new start," Pope Francis writes. Let's hope, for all our sake, that he is right.

20

The Anthropocene spirit

Pope Francis's message in *Laudato Si'* isn't a new one, even for a pope. In 1991, Pope John Paul II offered a similarly provocative counterpoint to the too widely accepted view of man's domination of nature, in his encyclical letter *Centesimus Annus* or *Hundredth Year*:

> Man thinks he can make arbitrary use of the earth, subjecting it without restraint to his will, as though it did not have its own requisites and a prior God-given purpose, which man can indeed develop but must not betray.[93]

Unlike his predecessor, however, Pope Francis has elevated concern for the environment in an encyclical letter all its own—an unprecedented occurrence in the history of Catholicism. But why now? The modern environmental movement has been with us for more than 50 years, leading to social movements, myriad legislation, and lifestyle changes that reflect environmentalists' modern focus on sustainability. Why does the pope's encyclical on ecology resonate so much today? What makes it the right message at the right time? Why are we called to create a sustainable world now more than ever before?

I believe the reason is one that I've touched on elsewhere in this book. We are at a unique moment in our time on Earth as a species, one never faced before and one requiring a new system of ethics, values, beliefs, worldviews, and, above all, spirituality. The pope's landmark encyclical provides a moral compass to help navigate the Anthropocene era.

In terms of science, acknowledging an unprecedented shift in our geophysical reality amounts to a significant moment in history. But the social and cultural shift is even more profound. Recognition of the Anthropocene demands that we act with an urgency and complexity that the currently dominant vision of sustainable development lacks. According to geographer and political philosopher Rory Rowan:

> The Anthropocene is not a problem for which there can be a solution. Rather, it names an emergent set of geo-social conditions that already fundamentally structure the horizon of human existence. It is thus not a new factor that can be accommodated within existing conceptual frameworks, including those within which policy is developed, but signals a profound shift in the human relation to the planet that questions the very foundations of these frameworks themselves.[94]

Droughts, wildfires, food insecurity, water scarcity, and the social unrest that results are all emergent markers of the Anthropocene Era that point to a fundamental system failure in the way we have designed our society. A response to the Anthropocene calls for a new set of societal values and beliefs about our relationship with ourselves, with each other, with the environment, and, for many, with God.

This will not go down easily. It demands a transformative cultural shift that is akin to the Enlightenment of the 17th and 18th centuries, when humankind went from seeing human endeavor as subsumed by nature to embarking on the "conquest of nature," under the metaphor of the planet as an enemy to be subdued.

In similar ways, the Anthropocene is an acknowledgment that the scientific method essential to the Enlightenment is no longer fully adequate to understand the natural world and our place in it. As Pope Francis points out:

> Given the complexity of the ecological crisis and its multiple causes, we need to realize that the solutions will not emerge from just one way of interpreting and transforming reality . . . If we are truly concerned to develop an ecology capable of remedying the damage we have done, no branch of the sciences and no form of wisdom can be left out, and that includes religion and the language particular to it.

In responding to the "urgent challenge to protect our common home," he asks us "to bring the whole human family together to seek a sustainable and integral development." This kind of global common cause is a challenge we have not yet faced as a species. It will demand a global set of ethics and values around collective responsibility and social equity that we do not yet know. For example, the fossil fuels burned in Ann Arbor, Shanghai, or Moscow have an equal impact on the global environment we all share, and therefore compel a common set of values about their emission. Addressing this problem will require the most complicated and intrusive global agreements ever negotiated. The kind of cooperation necessary to solve this problem is far beyond anything that we, as a species, have ever accomplished before. International treaties to ban land mines or eliminate ozone-depleting substances pale in comparison.

Pope Francis is trying to help us see this. Many have compared his letter to the 1891 encyclical letter *Rerum Novarum* or *Rights and Duties of Capital and Labor*, in which Pope Leo XIII addressed the condition of the working classes. In offering a spiritual way to understand the unprecedented confusion of clashing capitalist and communist notions of labor in the midst of the industrial revolution, *Rerum Novarum* has become a foundational document for Catholic social teaching.

Will *Laudato Si'* offer a similarly transformative way to understand the unprecedented confusion over global-scale environmental and social changes that we are creating? The answer to that question will not solely be a testament to the encyclical letter's importance; it will be a testament to our ability to hear a message that is hard to hear, and harder still to act upon. As Stephen Jay Gould wrote in 1985:

> We have become, by the power of a glorious evolutionary accident called intelligence, the stewards of life's continuity on earth. We did not ask for this role, but we cannot abjure it. We may not be suited to it, but here we are.[95]

Pope Francis is asking us to face this new reality with respect for the natural world around us and a humility to recognize our limitations in understanding how it works and what we are doing to it. He is asking this at a key moment in time when we are taking a new place in the natural world, or what he is careful to call "creation"—our spiritual home.

21

Conclusion: The Great Work

My goal in this book is to inspire people to pursue their personal passions and find a purpose in their work that they deeply connect with. I want to inspire people to find a calling, to be authentic in how they live their lives. I hope that these chapters have inspired you, challenged you, made you uncomfortable and, at times, even antagonized you. A calling is not easy; indeed, a calling is hard.

But we need your callings now more than ever. The responsibility we face as individuals and as a society to steward our planetary ecosystem represents the great challenge of today's generation, and possibly the greatest challenge of any generation. The environmental theologian Thomas Berry has called it *The Great Work*, and the title of this final chapter is in homage to his 1999 book. The sentiment in this passage, in particular, is never far from my mind:

> The success or failure of any historical age is the extent to which those living at that time have fulfilled the special

> role that history has imposed upon them. No age lives completely unto itself. Each age has only what it received from the prior generations. Just now we have abundant evidence that the various species of life, the mountains and rivers, and even the vast ocean itself, which once we thought beyond serious impact from humans, will survive only in their damaged integrity. The Great Work before us, the task of moving modern industrial civilization from its present devastating influence on the Earth to a more benign mode of presence, is not a role that we have chosen. It is a role given to us, beyond any consultation with ourselves. We did not choose. We were chosen by some power beyond ourselves for this historical task . . . We are, as it were, thrown into existence with a challenge and a role that is beyond any personal choice. The nobility of our lives, however, depends upon the manner in which we come to understand and fulfill our assigned role.[96]

That great challenge is now yours. The previous generation left the present and future generations with new problems that may seem insurmountable and new solutions that at times seem to be half measures. We can now see more clearly that the "more benign mode of presence" that Berry asked us to seek for ourselves on the Earth must nonetheless be an active mode, one that works in harmony with nature, seeking to positively steward environmental systems rather than simply lessening our impact. Where Berry saw environmental insults at the close of the twentieth century, we now see unavoidable environmental control within the age of the Anthropocene.

It is a completely different context, and the current generation has every right to be angry at this Great Work being thrust upon them. That said, there is no choice but to respond and we do not have the luxury of asking if our response will work, for we are at a place in human history never before seen. We don't know the answers or often even how to construct the answers, but we must try. The "nobility of our lives" will be determined by that effort.

Part of that effort is that we must work with those who cannot see the challenge before us. Despite our celebration of the relentless parade of seemingly new technologies, we remain a society and species that recoils from profound change. We can be selfish; we avoid facing difficult realities; we crucify those who force us to look. From Galileo Galilei to Rachel Carson to contemporary climate scientists, all were ridiculed, attacked, and at least initially dismissed by societies threatened by their seeing the truth. To take up sustainability as a vocation is to invite animosity.

Here, I find it helpful to remember two quotations. The first is from the actor Paul Newman: "If you don't have enemies, you don't have character."[97] Yet the animosity you face may in fact be fear or ignorance, a form of resistance that requires compassion and enlightenment. As John F. Kennedy warned more than 60 years ago, "The great enemy of truth is very often not the lie—deliberate, contrived, and dishonest—but the myth—persistent, persuasive, and unrealistic."[98]

This generation's Great Work calls us to convince the indifferent, the disengaged, the cautious, the fearful, the skeptical, and the openly antagonistic that the world has indeed changed, that we as humans occupy a new place within the environment, one that will determine the fate of the human project that has stood for millennia.

As you commence your life's work, start small, take that first step from where you are. Don't take it with the goal of changing the world—how you do that is not up to you. Instead, start your personal journey. You have no idea where it will take you. Screw in an LED light bulb, recycle your toilet paper roll, change your diet, read a book, take a course, think about what you consume, shift your career, challenge a politician. Begin to build your life's work, and connect it to The Great Work. This is a process, and properly taken, it leads to an outcome that you cannot predict.

We all have a role to play in this world and must undertake the task of discovering what it is with a mind open to the possibilities. The solutions to our collective problems will not be found in one worldview, one discipline, or one profession. Indeed, such narrow thinking is the great enemy of a calling.

For example, in my own journey I did not set out to become an academic, and yet here I am. But I choose to be the kind of academic I believe I must be; I am defining the role, and therefore my calling, for myself. I see great power in academia, and great limitations. I live in a world that respects data and analysis above all else, and yet I know that much in this world cannot be measured. You cannot show me data that proves that love for another human being, spiritual connection with the natural world, or the presence of God all exist. And yet I, and a great many people believe—or even know—they exist. I also live in a world that seeks to understand the natural world by breaking it down into its elemental parts and understanding each of its components. It has great difficulty understanding the interrelationships and interdependence of the whole, what Rachel Carson called the "web of life," and yet I know that the integrity of that whole is what is most important.[99] Finally, I live in a world that seeks to explain all phenomena through words and rational thought. And yet I know that a classical pianist or a professional athlete would have great difficulty in articulating the essence of their experience when they are perfecting their craft. This very book, for example, is intended to educate, as many academic books do. But it has no data, no models, and very few numbers.

It is also intended to challenge and inspire, something more academics should do.

Do these limitations diminish the role of academic that I have adopted? No, they strengthen that role, inspiring me to fill in the empty places with own sense of what an academic can and should be. My calling is to be an authentic academic, true to myself and the world as I see it. I choose not to be, to borrow a metaphor from Herbert Shepard, a "cormorant"—good at a particular skill (catching fish), but using that skill to serve another's purpose (the fisherman who ties a rope to the cormorant's foot, and takes the fish for himself).

Jim March, an emeritus professor at Stanford University, has been an extremely influential model of an intellectual to me. Jim is widely cited, has received many awards, and also has written nine books of poetry and two films. I first met Jim in 1995 at a small seminar at MIT while I was a graduate student. I asked him what he would teach if he were given the chance to teach anything. He smiled, and with great enthusiasm told me that he had recently been given that opportunity, and had chosen to teach management by way of the literary classics. I have never forgotten how excited he was as he told us all that the most important book that business students could read was *Don Quixote*. In a 2014 interview with *Insights by Stanford Business*, he explained:

> Quixote is hardly a good model for leadership, but he provides a basis for thinking about what justifies great action. Why do we do what we do? Our standard answer is that we do what we do because we expect it to lead to good consequences. Quixote reminds us that there is another possible answer: We do what we do because it fulfills our identity, our sense of self. Identity-based actions protect us from the discouragement of disappointing feedback. Of course, the cost is that it also slows learning. Both types of

> actions are essential elements of human sensibility, but our usual conversations—particularly in business settings and schools—tend to forget the second . . . We live in a world that emphasizes realistic expectations and clear successes. Quixote had neither. But through failure after failure, he persists in his vision and his commitment. He persists because he knows who he is.[100]

This is the essence of a calling. Have a vision, see a reality, and make it so, even when those around you (like those around Don Quixote) think it is foolish or crazy. You may fail, but you will learn who you are and be your own person.

Henry Ford failed and went broke five times before he succeeded. When Steve Jobs started Apple Computer in the mid-1970s and predicted a day when every home would have a computer, I, like many of my friends and colleagues at the time, thought it an absurd idea. Look out your window at the telephone poles that line your street. Now think back to the late nineteenth century and imagine someone predicting that we would install a 40-foot wooden pole every 120 feet along every street in the country. Consider the way that we now accept those poles as a part of the landscape. Now take note that they were first considered so offensive an urban blight that, in 1889, the *New York Times* reported a "War on Telephone Poles." Eula Biss wrote in *Harper's Magazine* that some homeowners and business owners cut them down as soon as they were erected. Some people defended their sidewalks with rifles. Property owners in Red Bank, New Jersey, threatened to tar and feather the workers who were putting up telephone poles. City governments in Sioux Falls, South Dakota, and Oshkosh, Wisconsin, ordered policemen to cut down all the poles in town. The Bell Telephone Company was forced to station a man atop every new pole to prevent any more chopping. And now we accept them as "natural." Who could have predicted that?

My grandmother, Christina Johanna Schneider, was born in 1894 and died in 1990. In the course of her lifetime, the Wright Brothers first flew, indoor plumbing and home electrification became common, the Ford Model T debuted, the first jet engine was developed, man landed on the moon and the computer age had begun. At her funeral, I thought that no generation would see the kinds of changes that she witnessed. But I now think I was wrong. The average child born today in the United States will live to the year 2094 and many will live into the twenty-second century. How different will that world be? And, importantly, what role will these children take in creating the world that they want to live in?

Nobel laureate Dennis Gabor once wrote that "the future cannot be predicted, but futures can be invented."[101] The future is there to do with as you wish. Be true to yourself, be authentic, be open to the possibilities of your life's work as they reveal themselves, and, in the words of Henry David Thoreau, you will "meet with a success unexpected in common hours."[102]

Acknowledgments

I would like to thank J.B. MacKinnon for helping me turn a series of essays into a more comprehensible narrative. His editing helped me draw out my ideas in a way that is far more clear and approachable than I had originally envisioned.

I would also like to thank my many co-authors—John Ehrenfeld, Dev Jennings, Max Bazerman, Marc Ventresca, Willie Ocasio, Lance Sandelands, Terry Nelidov, Jalal, Stephanie Bertels, Tima Bansal, Susse Georg, Rebecca Henn, John Woody, Judith Walls, Lianne Lefsrud, Melissa Wooten, Nitin Joglekar, Charles Corbett, Peter Wells, Nardia Haigh, Krista Badiane, Jennifer Howard-Grenville, Kim Wade-Benzoni, Leigh Thompson, Don Moore, James Gillespie, Steve Yaffee, Hannah Riley, Jack Troast, Patricia Misutka, Charlotte Coleman, Jenna White, and C.B. Bhattacharya. I am proud to have such a list of collaborators, all of whom have helped to form who I am as an academic, an intellectual and a person.

Finally, I would like to thank the many students that I have had the pleasure to know over 20-plus years of teaching. They have challenged and inspired me to keep exploring the answers to the great sustainability questions of our day and have helped me to test those ideas as I have undertaken this journey.

To all these people, and many more, I offer my thanks for helping me in my quest for a personal calling in environmental stewardship.

In building this book, I drew some materials from work that I had previously published. The following publications were adapted for use in the chapters of this book:

I. Life's Work as a Personal Vocation

- "Finding hope for a sustainable world." *Perspective: Sustainability Blog from the Erb Institute*, December 10 (2012). © Andrew Hoffman (Chapter 2).
- "Reflections on a theory of change." *Perspective: Sustainability Blog from the Erb Institute*, December 18 (2013). © Andrew Hoffman (Chapter 3).
- "Finding your model of leadership and change." *Perspective: Sustainability Blog from the Erb Institute*, April 17 (2015). © Andrew Hoffman (Chapter 4).
- "It's not just what you know; it's what you believe." *Perspective: Sustainability Blog from the Erb Institute*, May 1 (2015). © Andrew Hoffman (Chapter 5).
- "Valuing economy and environment: Why we care." *Triple Pundit*, July 1 (2014). Used with permission (Chapter 6).

II. Green Business as a Calling

- "The optimistic environmentalist." *Carbon Business*, Spring, 14-16 (2008). © Andrew Hoffman (Chapter 7).
- "Business must drive the social debate over climate change." *The Planet Blue Conversation*, January 24 (2014). © Andrew Hoffman (Chapter 7).
- "If you're not at the table, you're on the menu." *Harvard Business Review*, October, 34-35 (2007). Excerpted and reprinted with permission from "Climate Business/ Business Climate" by Michael E. Porter; Forest Reinhardt; Peter Schwartz; Daniel C. Esty; Alyson Slater; Christina Bortz; Andrew J. Hoffman; Auden Schendler; Vicki Bakhshi; Alexis Krajeski; Theodore Roosevelt; John Llewellyn; Maria Emilia Correa; Mark Way; Britta Rendlen. Harvard Business Review, October 2007. Copyright © 2007 by Harvard Business Publishing; all rights reserved. (Chapter 8).
- "Climate change: Triggering an early strike on CO_2." *Corporate Responsibility Officer*, March/April, 48-49 (2008). Used with permission; thank you to SharedXpertise Media, LLC, publisher of *Corporate Responsibility Magazine* (Chapter 8).
- "The wrong-headed solutions of corporate sustainability." *Greenbiz*, April 10 (2013) (with John Ehrenfeld). Used with permission. Adapted from *Flourishing: A Frank Conversation about Sustainability*, by John R. Ehrenfeld and Andrew J. Hoffman, copyright © 2013 by the Board of Trustees of the Leland Stanford Jr. University. All rights reserved. Reprinted by permission of

the publisher, Stanford University Press, sup.org (Chapter 9).

- "Sustainability in the global marketplace: Our global future in the Anthropocene." *Triple Pundit*, November 5 (2013) (with Jalal and Terry Nelidov). Used with permission (Chapters 9 and 13).
- "Sustainability in the global marketplace: Business-almost-as-usual." *Triple Pundit*, October 29 (2013) (with Jalal and Terry Nelidov). Used with permission (Chapters 9 and 13).
- "Sustainability 2.0: Sustainability is dead, long live sustainability." *Solutions*, 4(3) (June) (2013) (with John Ehrenfeld). Used with permission. Adapted from *Flourishing: A Frank Conversation about Sustainability*, by John R. Ehrenfeld and Andrew J. Hoffman. Copyright © 2013 by the Board of Trustees of the Leland Stanford Jr. University. All rights reserved. Reprinted by permission of the publisher, Stanford University Press, sup.org (Chapters 9 and 11).
- "Capitalism must evolve to solve climate crisis." *The Conversation*, September 16 (2015). Used with permission, *The Conversation* (Chapter 10).
- "Are you green? Yes? But how 'dark' or 'bright' green is that?" *Our Values*, April 27 (2009). Used with permission, Our Values.org (Chapter 11).

III. Reclaiming the Role of Academia

- "Isolated scholars: Making bricks, not shaping policy." *The Chronicle of Higher Education*, February 9 (2015). © Andrew Hoffman (Chapter 12).
- "The balancing act: Public engagement for the academic scholar." *The Union of Concerned Scientists, The Equation*, November 5 (2013). Used with permission, Union of Concerned Scientists. (Chapters 12 and 13).
- "Are academic scholars 'lost to the academy'? A call for more public intellectuals in the climate change debate." *Network for Business Sustainability blog*, January 16 (2012). Used with permission, Network for Business Sustainability (Chapters 12 and 13).
- Hoffman, A., *et al.* (2015) *Academic Engagement in Public and Political Discourse: Proceedings of the Michigan Meeting, May 2015* (Ann Arbor, MI: Michigan Publishing). Used with permission, Michigan Publishing (Chapter 13).
- "A renewed focus and tone for O&NE scholarship." *Organizations and the Natural Environment Blog*, March 27 (2015) (with Dev Jennings). © Andrew Hoffman and Dev Jennings (Chapter 14).

IV. Changing Culture and Values

- "The limits of carbon pricing: Can high prices alone cut emissions?" *Business Week,* November 18 (2009). Used with permission, Bloomberg Content Services. (Chapter 15).

- "The cultural schism of climate change: How science takes a back seat to identity politics in the U.S." *Stanford University Press blog*, October 24 (2014). Used with permission. Adapted from *How Culture Shapes the Climate Change Debate*, by Andrew J. Hoffman. Copyright © 2015 by the Board of Trustees of the Leland Stanford Jr. University. All rights reserved. Reprinted by permission of the publisher, Stanford University Press, sup.org (Chapter 16).
- "Don't ignore climate skeptics. Talk to them differently." *Christian Science Monitor*, June 24 (2011). © Andrew Hoffman (Chapter 16).
- "Social sciences are best hope for ending debates over climate change." *The Conversation*, April 2 (2015). Used with permission, *The Conversation* (Chapter 17).
- "Climate change's poisoned culture." *Geographical*, February 5 (2015). Used with permission, *Geographical* (Chapter 17).

V. A Call to a Calling

- "The Pope as messenger: Making climate change a moral issue." *The Conversation,* April 10 (2015) (with Jenna White). Used with permission, *The Conversation* (Chapter 18).
- "Pope encyclical on 'ecological crisis' asks us to examine our deepest values and beliefs." *The Conversation,* June 18 (2015). Used with permission, *The Conversation* (Chapters 18 and 19).

- "The pope's encyclical letter and its implications for business." *Environment*, October (2015). Used with permission, Taylor & Francis (Chapter 19).
- "The pope, climate change and the cultural dimensions of the Anthropocene." *The Conversation,* July 17 (2015). Used with permission, *The Conversation* (Chapter 20).

Biographies

Photo: Mike Gould

Andrew J. Hoffman is the Holcim (U.S.) Professor of Sustainable Enterprise at the University of Michigan, a position that holds joint appointments at the Stephen M. Ross School of Business and the School of Natural Resources & Environment. He also serves as Education Director of the Graham Sustainability Institute. Hoffman has written extensively about the processes by which environmental issues both emerge and evolve as social, political, and managerial issues. He has published over 100 articles and book chapters as well as 14 books, two of which have been translated into five languages. He has been awarded the Maggie Award (2013), JMI Breaking the Frame Award (2012), Connecticut Book Award (2011), the Aldo Leopold Fellowship (2011), the Aspen Environmental Fellowship (2011 and 2009), the Manos Page Prize (2009), the Faculty Pioneer Award (2003), the Rachel Carson Book Prize (2001), and the Klegerman Award

(1995). His work has been covered in the *New York Times*, *The Atlantic*, *Scientific American*, *Time*, the *Wall Street Journal*, and National Public Radio. Prior to academics, Hoffman worked as a general contractor of custom estates and as an inspector for the US EPA. He earned his PhD in both Management and Civil & Environmental Engineering at MIT. He lives in Ann Arbor, Michigan.

Photo: A. Smith

J.B. MacKinnon is a journalist and author or co-author of four books of non-fiction. His latest, *The Once and Future World*, won the 2014 Green Prize for Sustainable Literature. His previous works include *The 100-Mile Diet* (with Alisa Smith), a bestseller widely recognized as a catalyst of the local foods movement. As a journalist, MacKinnon has won more than a dozen national and international awards in categories as varied as essays, science writing, and travelogue. His work appears in major outlets such as *The New Yorker* and *National Geographic*, as well as vanguard publications such as *Orion* and *Adbusters*, the "culture jamming" magazine that launched the Occupy movement. His stories have ranged from the civil war in South Sudan to anarchists in urban North America to the overlooked world of old age among wild animals. MacKinnon lives with his partner, Alisa Smith, in Vancouver, Canada.

Endnotes

Epigraph

1. H.D. Thoreau (1854). *Walden*. Boston, MA: Ticknor & Fields.

1. Introduction: finding purpose

2. Ibid.
3. J.D. Campbell (1988). *Joseph Campbell and the Power of Myth*. New York: Doubleday & Co.
4. H. Shepard (1984). On realization of human potential: A path with a heart. In M. Arthur, L. Bailyn, D. Levinson, & H. Shepard (Eds.), *Working with Careers* (pp. 25-46). New York: Center for Research on Careers, Graduate School of Business, Columbia University.

2. Finding hope

5. V. Havel (1985). *The Power of the Powerless*. Armonk, NY: M.E. Sharpe.
6. C. Lasch, (1978). *The Culture of Narcissism: American Life in an Era of Diminished Expectations*. New York: W.W. Norton.
7. D. Orr (1994). *Earth in Mind: On Education, Environment and the Human Prospect*. Washington, DC: Island Press.
8. B. Crosette (1998, September 27). Kofi Annan's astonishing facts. *New York Times*. Retrieved from: www.nytimes.com/learning/general/featured_articles/980928monday.html

9. A. Saunders (2011, March 1). The MT interview: Paul Polman of Unilever. *Management Today*. Retrieved from: www.managementtoday.co.uk/features/1055793
10. D.D. Eisenhower (1961, January 17). Eisenhower's farewell address to the nation. Retrieved from: mcadams.posc.mu.edu/ike.htm
11. D. Headstrong (2007). *From Telegraph to Light Bulb with Thomas Edison*. Nashville, TN: B&H Publishing Group.

3. Your theory of change

12. I. Shenkar (1967, July 11). E.B. White: Notes and comment by the author. *New York Times*. Retrieved from: https://www.nytimes.com/books/97/08/03/lifetimes/white-notes.html
13. J.F. Kennedy (1962, June 11). *Yale University Commencement Address*, New Haven CT. Retrieved from: millercenter.org/president/speeches/speech-3370
14. R. Williams (1989). *Resources of Hope: Culture, Democracy, Socialism*. Brooklyn, NY: Verso.
15. M. Shellenberger & T. Nordhaus (2004). *The Death of Environmentalism: Global Warming in a Post-Environmental World*. Oakland, CA: The Breakthrough Institute. Retrieved from: thebreakthrough.org/archive/the_death_of_environmentalism
16. Shenkar, *op. cit.*

4. Your model of leadership

17. A. Leiserowitz, E. Maibach, C. Roser-Renouf, & G. Feinberg (2013). How Americans communicate about global warming in April 2013. Yale University and George Mason University. New Haven, CT: Yale Project on Climate Change Communication. Retrieved from: environment.yale.edu/climate-communication/article/how-americans-communicate-about-global-warming-april-2013
18. J. Pfeffer (1992). *Managing with Power: Politics and Influence in Organizations*. Boston, MA: Harvard Business School Press.
19. J.B. MacKinnon (2014, November). The incredible lightness of being arrested. *Orion Magazine*. Retrieved from: https://orionmagazine.org/2014/11/the-incredible-lightness-of-being-arrested

5. What do you believe?

20. The Discovery Channel (2013). *North America*. Retrieved from: www.discovery.com/tv-shows/north-america
21. R. Carson (1955). *The Edge of the Sea*. Boston, MA: Houghton Mifflin.

6. Why do you care?

22. R. Pirsig (1974). *Zen and the Art of Motorcycle Maintenance: An Inquiry into Values*. New York: Morrow Publishing.
23. K. Burns (2009). *The National Parks: America's Best Idea*. Washington, DC: Public Broadcasting System.

7. Why green business?

24. Associated Press (2015, November 10). Apple boss pushes business to help solve social problems. *Associated Press*. Retrieved from: bigstory.ap.org/article/020c232107764e85850d3fc5bb6b4a71/apple-ceo-says-businesses-must-help-solve-climate-change
25. C. Davenport (2014, January 23). Industry awakens to threat of climate change. *International New York Times*. Retrieved from: www.nytimes.com/2014/01/24/science/earth/threat-to-bottom-line-spurs-action-on-climate.html?_r=0

8. Green in the corner office

26. U.S. Green Building Council (2015). Green building facts. Retrieved from: www.usgbc.org/articles/green-building-facts
27. A. McCrone, U. Moslener, E. Usher, C. Grüning, & V. Sonntag-O'Brien (Eds) (2015). *Global Trends in Renewable Energy Investments 2015*. Frankfurt, Germany: UN Environment Programme.
28. D. Saha (2014). Galvanize foreign direct investment in U.S. clean energy. Washington, DC: Brookings Institution. Retrieved from: www.brookings.edu/blogs/the-avenue/posts/2014/12/19-foreign-direct-investment-clean-energy-saha
29. U.S. Energy Information Administration (2015). *Annual Energy Outlook 2015 with Projections to 2040*. Washington, DC: U.S. Energy Information Administration. Retrieved from: www.eia.gov/forecasts/aeo
30. C. Davenport (2015, November 27). Bill Gates expected to create billion-dollar fund for clean energy. *New York Times*. Retrieved from: www.

nytimes.com/2015/11/28/us/politics/bill-gates-expected-to-create-billion-dollar-fund-for-clean-energy.html?_r=0

31. K.A. Strassel (2007, January 26). If the cap fits. *Wall Street Journal.*
32. U.S. Department of Health (1964). Smoking and Health. Report of the Advisory Committee to the Surgeon General of the Public Health Service. PHS Publication No. 1103. Washington, DC: U.S. Department of Health, Education and Welfare.
33. *Automotive News* (2007, April 27). Ford tackles climate change. *Automotive News*. Retrieved from: autonews.gasgoo.com/global-news/ford-tackles-climate-change-070425.shtml
34. A. Hoffman (2006). Getting ahead of the curve: Corporate strategies that address climate change. Pew Center on Climate Change. Arlington, VA: C2ES. Retrieved from: www.c2es.org/publications/getting-ahead-curve-corporate-strategies-address-climate-change
35. Ibid.
36. Ibid.
37. A. Hoffman (2008). Climate change: Triggering an early strike on CO_2. *Corporate Responsibility Officer*, March/April, 48-49. Retrieved from: www.thecro.com/topics/environment/triggering-an-early-strike-on-co2
38. T. Henneman (2011, November 5). Patagonia fills payroll with people who are passionate. *Workforce*. Retrieved from: www.workforce.com/articles/patagonia-fills-payroll-with-people-who-are-passionate
39. JP Morgan (2014). New J.P. Morgan & GIIN survey indicates higher impact investment commitments, investor satisfaction. New York: JP Morgan Chase & Co.

9. Business (almost) as usual

40. S.F. Fitzgerald, (1936, April). The crack up. *Esquire*. Reprinted in 2008. Retrieved from: www.esquire.com/news-politics/a4310/the-crack-up
41. World Commission on Environment and Development (1987). *Our Common Future*. New York: United Nations.
42. J. Ehrenfeld, & A. Hoffman (2013). *Flourishing: A Frank Conversation on Sustainability*. Palo Alto, CA: Stanford University Press.

10. Capitalism and markets must evolve

43. Buttonwood (2014, November 15). All it needs is love. Capitalism's reputation badly damaged by the bankers. *The Economist*. Retrieved

from: www.economist.com/news/finance-and-economics/21632602-capitalisms-reputation-has-been-damaged-bankers-all-it-needs-love

44. Y. Levin (2010, January 11). Recovering the case for capitalism. *National Affairs,* 3. Retrieved from: www.nationalaffairs.com/publications/detail/recovering-the-case-for-capitalism
45. A. Giridharadas (2015). The Thriving World, the Wilting World and You. Keynote address, 2015 Aspen Action Forum. Retrieved from: www.aspeninstitute.org/video/anand-giridharadas-thriving-world-wilting-world-you
46. E. Beinhicker & N. Hanauer (2014, September). Redefining capitalism. *McKinsey Quarterly.* Retrieved from: www.mckinsey.com/insights/corporate_social_responsibility/redefining_capitalism
47. L. Stout (2012). The problem of corporate purpose. *Issues in Governance Studies.* Washington, DC: Brookings Institution. Retrieved from: www.brookings.edu/research/papers/2012/06/18-corporate-stout
48. P. Polman (2014, May). Business, society, and the future of capitalism. *McKinsey Quarterly.* Retrieved from: www.mckinsey.com/insights/sustainability/business_society_and_the_future_of_capitalism
49. N. Klein (2011, November 9). Capitalism versus the climate. *The Nation.* Retrieved from: www.thenation.com/article/capitalism-vs-climate
50. S.J. Gould (1989, November). The creation myths of Cooperstown. *Natural History.* Retrieved from: www.naturalhistorymag.com/picks-from-the-past/02484/the-creation-myths-of-cooperstown

11. Dark green or light green?

51. A. Steffen (2009, February 27). Bright green, light green, dark green, gray: The new environmental spectrum. *Worldchanging.* Retrieved from: www.worldchanging.com/archives/009499.html
52. D. Meadows, J. Randers & D. Meadows (1992). *Beyond the Limits: Confronting Global Collapse, Envisioning a Sustainable Future.* White River Junction, VT: Chelsea Green Publishing Co.
53. A. Leopold (1949). *A Sand County Almanac, and Sketches Here and There.* Oxford, UK: Oxford University Press.

12. Making bricks versus making change

54. B.K. Forscher (1963, October 18). Chaos in the brickyard. *Science*, 142(339). Retrieved from: warnercnr.colostate.edu/~anderson/PDF_files/Chaos.pdf
55. R. Jacoby (2000). *The Last Intellectuals: American Culture in the Age of Academe*. New York: Basic Books.
56. A. Hoffman *et al.* (2015). *Academic Engagement in Public and Political Discourse: Proceedings of the Michigan Meeting, May 2015*. Ann Arbor, MI: Michigan Publishing.
57. L. Rainie, C. Funk & M. Anderson (2015, February 15). *How Scientists Engage the Public*. Washington, DC: Pew Research Center. Retrieved from: www.pewinternet.org/2015/02/15/how-scientists-engage-public
58. J. Besley & M. Nisbet (2013). How scientists view the public, the media and the political process, *Public Understanding of Science*, 22(6), 644-659. Retrieved from: pus.sagepub.com/content/early/2011/08/26/09636 62511418743
59. L. Hamilton (2011). *Do You Believe the Climate is Changing?* Durham, NY: Carsey Institute, University of New Hampshire. Retrieved from: scholars.unh.edu/cgi/viewcontent.cgi?article=1153&context=carsey
60. R. Goldman (2010, May 3). Limbaugh, scientists square off on oil spill cleanup. *ABC News*. Retrieved from: abcnews.go.com/Technology/limbaugh-environmentalists-square-off-blame-oil-leak/story?id=10542582
61. M. Burawoy (2005). For public sociology. *American Sociological Review*, 70, 4-28. Retrieved from: burawoy.berkeley.edu/Public%20Sociology,%20Live/Burawoy.pdf

13. Public engagement as a balancing act

62. Hoffman *et al.*, *op cit.*
63. K. Tippett (2009, February 12). *Transcript for David Brooks and E.J. Dionne—Obama's Theologian: Reinhold Niebuhr and the American Present*. On Being with Krista Tippett. Retrieved from: www.onbeing.org/program/obama039s-theologian-david-brooks-and-ej-dionne-reinhold-niebuhr-and-american-present-7
64. Times Higher Education (2011, March 31). Citation averages, 2000–2010, by fields and years. *Times Higher Education*. Retrieved from: https://www.timeshighereducation.com/news/citation-averages-2000-2010-by-fields-and-years/415643.article

65. J. West (2012, January 13). MIT climate scientist's wife threatened in a "frenzy of hate." *Mother Jones*. Retrieved from: www.motherjones.com/environment/2012/01/mit-climate-scientists-wife-threatened-frenzy-hate

14. The new environmental scholarship

66. P. Crutzen (2002). Geology of mankind. *Nature*, 415, 23. Retrieved from: www.nature.com/nature/journal/v415/n6867/full/415023a.html
67. J. Rockström *et al.* (2009). Planetary boundaries: Exploring the safe operating space for humanity. *Ecology and Society*, 14(2), 32. Retrieved from: www.ecologyandsociety.org/vol14/iss2/art32
68. T. Gladwin (2012). Capitalism critique: Systemic limits on business harmony with nature. In P. Bansal & A. Hoffman (Eds.). *The Oxford Handbook of Business and the Environment* (pp. 657-674). Oxford, UK: Oxford University Press.
69. R. Khurana (2007). *From Higher Aims to Hired Hands: The Social Transformation of American Business Schools and the Unfulfilled Promise of Management as a Profession*. Princeton, NJ: Princeton University Press.
70. D. Meyerson & M. Scully (1995). Tempered radicalism and the politics of ambivalence and change. *Organization Science*, 6, 585-600.

15. Culture and carbon

16. Culture and climate

71. R. Limbaugh (2014, January 6). Left creates "polar vortex" to make you think winter is caused by global warming. The Rush Limbaugh Show. Retrieved from: www.rushlimbaugh.com/daily/2014/01/06/left_creates_polar_vortex_to_make_you_think_winter_is_caused_by_global_warming
72. Fox News Weather Center (2014, January 7). "Polar vortex" breaks temperature records in southern and eastern parts of US. Fox News. Retrieved from: www.foxnews.com/weather/2014/01/08/polar-vortex-spreads-into-eastern-southern-us
73. G. Pollowitz (2014, January 7). Alarmists: Global warming may be causing polar vortex. *National Review*. Retrieved from: www.nationalreview.com/planet-gore/367779/alarmists-global-warming-may-be-causing-polar-vortex-greg-pollowitz

74. D. Kahan (2010). Fixing the communications failure. *Nature*, 463(21), 296-297. Retrieved from: www.nature.com/nature/journal/v463/n7279/full/463296a.html
75. A. McCright & R. Dunlap (2011). The politicization of climate change and polarization in the American public's views of global warming, 2001–2010. *The Sociological Quarterly*, 52, 155-194. Retrieved from: news.msu.edu/media/documents/2011/04/593fe28b-fbc7-4a86-850a-2fe029dbeb41.pdf
76. D. Kahan, E. Peters, M. Wittlin, P. Slovic, L. Ouellette, D. Braman, & G. Mandel (2012). The polarizing impact of science literacy and numeracy on perceived climate change risks. *Nature Climate Change*, 210, 732-735. Retrieved from: www.nature.com/nclimate/journal/v2/n10/full/nclimate1547.html
77. Pew Research Center (2014, January 27). *Climate Change: Key Data Points from Pew Research*. Washington, DC: Pew Research Center.

17. Detoxifying the climate change debate

78. E. Demaria (2015, March 22). California Governor Jerry Brown: Ted Cruz "unfit to be running" for President. NBC News. Retrieved from: www.nbcnews.com/meet-the-press/california-governor-ted-cruz-unfit-be-running-n328046
79. Phillips, A. (2015, March 23). Ted Cruz responds to Gov. Jerry Brown calling him 'absolutely unfit' to run for office. *Climate Progress*. Retrieved from: thinkprogress.org/climate/2015/03/23/3637430/ted-cruz-takes-on-jerry-brown
80. Erb Institute/Union of Concerned Scientists (2012). Increasing public understanding of climate risks and choices: Learning from social science research and practice. Ann Arbor, MI/Cambridge, MA: Erb Institute/Union of Concerned Scientists. Retrieved from: erb.umich.edu/Research/InstituteReports/11-12/UCS_ErbWorkshopReport.pdf
81. C. Mooney (2011, April 18). The science of why we don't believe science. *Mother Jones*. Retrieved from: www.motherjones.com/politics/2011/03/denial-science-chris-mooney
82. J. Haidt (2006). *The Happiness Hypothesis: Finding Modern Truth in Ancient Wisdom*. New York: Basic Books.
83. CNA (2014). National security and the accelerating risks of climate change. Alexandria, VA: CNA Military Advisory Board. Retrieved from: https://www.cna.org/cna_files/pdf/MAB_5-8-14.pdf

18. Pope Francis as messenger

84. Leopold, *op. cit.*
85. Pope Francis (2015). Encyclical letter *Laudato Si'*. Vatican City: Libreria Editrice Vaticana. Retrieved from: w2.vatican.va/content/francesco/en/encyclicals/documents/papa-francesco_20150524_enciclica-laudato-si.html
86. Yale Project on Climate Communication (2015). American Catholics worry about global warming and support U.S. action. New Haven, CT: Yale University. Retrieved from: environment.yale.edu/climate-communication/article/american-catholics-worry-about-global-warming-and-support-u.s.-action
87. D. Knowles (2015, March 24). Lindsey Graham blames Republicans (and Al Gore) for climate change inaction. *Bloomberg Politics*. Retrieved from: www.bloomberg.com/politics/articles/2015-03-24/lindsey-graham-blames-republicans-and-al-gore-for-climate-change-inaction
88. C. Davenport & M. Connelly (2015, January 30). Most Republicans say they back climate action, poll finds. *New York Times*. Retrieved from: www.nytimes.com/2015/01/31/us/politics/most-americans-support-government-action-on-climate-change-poll-finds.html
89. ClearPath (2015). Republicans, clean energy, and climate change. ClearPath. Retrieved from: https://polling.clearpath.org/docs/clearpath_survey_report.pdf
90. R. Riffkin (2014, March 12). Climate change not a top worry in the U.S. Gallup. Retrieved from: www.gallup.com/poll/167843/climate-change-not-top-worry.aspx

19. To till and keep the garden

91. L. White (1967, March 10). The historical roots of our ecological crisis. *Science*, 155(3767), 1,203-1,207. Retrieved from: science.sciencemag.org/content/155/3767/1203
92. D. Desilver (2013, December 5). U.S. income inequality, on rise for decades, is now highest since 1928. Washington, DC: Pew Research Center. Retrieved from: www.pewresearch.org/fact-tank/2013/12/05/u-s-income-inequality-on-rise-for-decades-is-now-highest-since-1928

20. The Anthropocene spirit

93. Pope John Paul II (1991). Encyclical letter *Centesimus Annus*. Vatican City: Libreria Editrice Vaticana. Retrieved from: w2.vatican.va/content/john-paul-ii/en/encyclicals/documents/hf_jp-ii_enc_01051991_centesimus-annus.html
94. R. Rowan (2014). Notes on politics after the Anthropocene. In E. Johnson & H. Morehouse (Eds.). *After the Anthropocene: Politics and Geographic Inquiry for a New Epoch* (pp. 9-12). *Progress in Human Geography*, 38(3), 439-441.
95. S.J. Gould (1991). *The Flamingo's Smile: Reflections in Natural History*. New York: Penguin Books.

21. Conclusion: The Great Work

96. T. Berry (2000). *The Great Work: Our Way into the Future*. New York: Bell Tower.
97. M. Farren (2004). *Words of Wisdom: From the Greatest Minds of All Time*. London: Robson Books Ltd.
98. Kennedy, *op. cit.*
99. R. Carson (1962). *Silent Spring*. Boston, MA: Houghton Mifflin.
100. L. Mooney (2014, February 19). James March: What Don Quixote teaches us about leadership. *Stanford Business*. Retrieved from: https://www.gsb.stanford.edu/insights/james-march-what-don-quixote-teaches-us-about-leadership
101. D. Gabor (1962). *Inventing the Future*. London: Secker & Warburg.
102. Thoreau, *op. cit.*

Also by Andrew J. Hoffman

Authored books

Academic Engagement in Public and Political Discourse (with Kirsti Ashworth, Chase Dwelle, Peter Goldberg, Andrew Henderson, Louis Merlin, Yulia Muzyrya, Norma-Jean Simon, Veronica Taylor, Corinne Weisheit, and Sarah Wilson)

How Culture Shapes the Climate Change Debate

Flourishing: A Frank Conversation about Sustainability (with John Ehrenfeld)

Climate Change: What's Your Business Strategy? (with John Woody)

Carbon Strategies: How Leading Companies are Reducing their Climate Change Footprint

From Heresy to Dogma: An Institutional History of Corporate Environmentalism

Competitive Environmental Strategy: A Guide to the Changing Business Landscape

Edited books

Constructing Green: The Social Structures of Sustainability (with Rebecca Henn)

Business and the Environment: Critical Perspectives on Business and Management (with Susse Georg)

The Oxford Handbook on Business and the Natural Environment (with Pratima Bansal)
Organizations, Policy and the Natural Environment: Institutional and Strategic Perspectives (with Marc Ventresca)
Global Climate Change: Senior Level Dialogue at the Intersection of Economics, Strategy, Technology, Science, Politics and International Negotiation

Memoir

Builder's Apprentice